# THE QUESTION
# OF WOMAN

# THE QUESTION OF WOMAN

*The Collected Writings of*
*Charlotte von Kirschbaum*

Translated by
John Shepherd

Edited and with an Introduction by
Eleanor Jackson

WILLIAM B. EERDMANS PUBLISHING COMPANY
GRAND RAPIDS, MICHIGAN / CAMBRIDGE, U.K.

Originally published as *Die wirkliche Frau*
© 1944 Evangelischer Verlag, Zollikon-Zurich
Appendix originally published as
*Der Dienst der Frau in der Wortverkündigung*
© 1951 Evangelischer Verlag, Zollikon-Zurich

English translation © 1996 Wm. B. Eerdmans Publishing Co.
255 Jefferson Ave. S.E., Grand Rapids, Michigan 49503 /
P.O. Box 163, Cambridge CB3 9PU U.K.
All rights reserved

Printed in the United States of America

01 00 99 98 97 96      7 6 5 4 3 2 1

**Library of Congress Cataloging-in-Publication Data**

Kirschbaum, Charlotte von, 1899-1975.
[Wirkliche Frau. English]
The question of woman : the collected writings of Charlotte von Kirschbaum /
translated by John Shepherd ; with an introduction by Eleanor Jackson.
p.      cm.
"Appendix originally published as Der Dienst der Frau in der
Wortverkündigung" — T.p. verso.
Includes bibliographical references.
ISBN 0-8028-4142-2 (pbk. : alk. paper)
1. Woman (Christian theology) 2. Kirschbaum, Charlotte von, 1899-1975. 3.
Barth, Karl, 1886-1968 — Friends and associates. I. Kirschbaum, Charlotte
von, 1899-1975. Dienst der Frau in der Wortverkündigung. English. II. Title.
BT704.K4713        1996
208'.2 — dc20                                        96-917
                                                        CIP

*In memoriam*
*A. David Lewis,*
*17 October 1916 to 28 August 1995,*
*a champion of women's rights and*
*a lifelong student of Karl Barth*

"All *mankinde* is of one *Author,* and is one *volume;*
when one Man dies, one *chapter* is not *torne* out of
the *booke,* but *translated* into a better *language;* and
every *chapter* must be so *translated;* God emploies
several *translators;* some peeces are translated by *age,*
some by *sicknesse,* some by *warre,* some by *justice;* but
*Gods* hand is in every *translation;* and his hand shall
bind up all our scattered leaves againe, for that *Librarie*
where every *booke* shall lie open to one another."

—John Donne, *Devotion XVII,* 1624

# CONTENTS

# ACKNOWLEDGMENTS

IT would have been impossible to produce this book without, in the first place, the creativity, courage, and scholarship of Charlotte von Kirschbaum herself, and I hope that this book is in some small way a fitting tribute to her. She herself would wish to pay tribute to her mentor and partner, Karl Barth, for his encouragement and for the evident use of his library. Second, one is indebted to John Shepherd for his patience in crafting such a fine translation of a difficult text, which required only minor technical embellishments, and to Michael Walpole for his diligence in searching for some of the more obscure quotations and references. Third, there was the generosity of Reverend Renate Köbler in making available to me her study, *Schattenarbeit: Charlotte von Kirschbaum, die Theologin an der Seite Karl Barths*, and the assistance of her publishers, Pahl-Rugenstein Verlag, Bonn, in tracing Charlotte von Kirschbaum's writings. I am especially indebted to Hartmut for procuring the photographs. Fourth, Dr. Edwin Robertson and Professor Charles Cranfield were helpful with their recollections, but all this would have been in vain had not Wm. B. Eerdmans and colleagues recognized the value of the book when other publishers preferred to stick to the orthodox view of Barth's work. Finally, there has been the role of my dear husband, Klaus Stoll, as agent provocateur and champion of Charlotte von Kirschbaum, in enabling this publication — a real *Gegenüber* (counterpart, protagonist, sparring partner, etc.). However, this book is dedicated not to him but to the memory of my uncle, David Lewis, who told me at Easter 1969 that if I wanted to be a theologian I must learn German and learn to type. I did, and this is the result. The quotation from John Donne on the work of a translator seems a fitting tribute to his life, and to that of Charlotte von Kirschbaum.

# INTRODUCTION

TO the casual reader of the *Church Dogmatics,* the following words by Karl Barth might seem to be no more than the conventional tribute to one's devoted secretary, even though couched in the language some writers use to describe their wife's forbearance: "I should not like to conclude this Preface without expressly drawing the attention of readers of these seven volumes to what they and I owe to the twenty years of work quietly accomplished at my side by Charlotte von Kirschbaum. She has devoted no less of her life and powers to the growth of this work than I have myself. Without her co-operation it could not have been advanced from day to day, and I should hardly dare contemplate the future which may yet remain to me. I know what it really means to have a helper" (*Church Dogmatics* [in references hereafter *CD*], III/3, trans. G. W. Bromiley and R. J. Ehrlich, ed. Bromiley and T. F. Torrance [Edinburgh: T. & T. Clark, 1960], pp. xii-xiii).

Charlotte von Kirschbaum was more than the untiring secretary, the compliant partner for life, or the inspired amanuensis. Trained as a Red Cross nurse and then as a secretary, self-taught in theology, she developed into a theologian in her own right, as recent examination of her long-neglected writings shows. It is important to study her life and reclaim her work, first, as this volume will show, because of the content of her work and the insight it provides into her times, especially the German church struggle and the early debates in World Council of Churches; second, because of its relevance today in the continuing debate about the ministry of women; and third, because a woman of her caliber should not be allowed to disappear into oblivion. One could as well ignore Hildegard of Bingen or the women pioneers of the ecumenical movement in her generation such as Madeleine Barot or Kathleen Bliss.

Women have become accustomed to the conspiracy of silence that has so often surrounded their achievements. Indeed, often, like von Kirschbaum, they have connived at it and, like the composer Gustav Mahler's wife, suppressed their own talents in the interests of their spouse's advancement. Nevertheless it is both frustrating and surprising that access to her work is difficult, even for those who read German. A few notable speeches, pamphlets, and lectures of hers are included in Renate Köbler's remarkable short biography *Schattenarbeit: Charlotte von Kirschbaum — Die Theologin an der Seite Karl Barths;*[1] although it is uncertain whether the American or the Dutch translations are still available, the German original itself is out of print. This is most unfortunate. Von Kirschbaum's own book, *Die wirkliche Frau,* was translated into Japanese soon after its original appearance by a Japanese doctoral student of Barth, and published in 1956, but has not been reprinted or translated into English until now. Only Eberhard Busch's monumental biography of Barth gives due credit and recognition for her work;[2] editions of Barth's work and books about his theology and ethics are still appearing without any mention of her. The paradox is that while

---

1. Renate Köbler, *Schattenarbeit: Charlotte von Kirschbaum — Die Theologin an der Seite Karl Barths* (Bonn: Pahl-Rugenstein, 1988). This is a thesis written for a first degree in theology, but it is remarkable for the interviews with von Kirschbaum's friends and members of the Barth family. It contains a stunning collection of family snapshots. I am indebted to Reverend Köbler for making the German edition of this book available to me.

2. Eberhard Busch, *Karl Barth: His Life from Letters and Autobiographical Texts,* trans. John Bowden (London: SCM, 1976). ET of *Karl Barths Lebenslauf: Nach seinen Briefen und autobiographischen Texten,* 2nd ed. (Munich: Kaiser, 1976).

2

many students today may consider Barth's theology out of date, von Kirschbaum's legacy still has relevance.

The first question is the extent to which her life and work can be disentangled from that of Barth. Who was the real Charlotte von Kirschbaum?

The second question concerns the principles that drove her and the self-awareness that sustained her. Why did she allow herself to be in an apparently impossible position for an independent-minded woman, in the eyes of the world? More radical in her stance on many issues than Barth, it requires a paradox worthy of his theology to understand her and interpret her life fairly. Much in her situation, as will be explained below, would call forth the righteous indignation of any woman, let alone that of feminist theologians, but to explain her story in feminist categories is to ignore the fact that she herself did not feel herself to be the victim of exploitation, and those who met her and knew her work deny that she was a shadowy figure engaged in "shadow work."[3] Despite her suffering, in her final years she made it clear she felt that she (and her friends) had had a good life.[4]

Third, there is the question of her theology, developed independently of Barth and yet interdependent. One can trace her hand in the *Church Dogmatics* and see how substantial her contribution was. Who was influencing whom? John Shepherd's admirable translation of her one substantive independent work, *Die wirkliche Frau*, allows one to judge how important her contribution was. What was the significance of her voice in her generation?

---

3. The Reverend Edwin Robertson, BBC program maker in the 1950s, makes this point most forcibly in the foreword he wrote for the Dutch translation of Köbler's book, *In de Schaduw van Karl Barth: Charlotte von Kirschbaum* (Kampen: Kok, 1991). In spite of this, Berthold Brecht's poem is quoted:

| | |
|---|---|
| Denn die einen sind im Dunkeln | Then some are in darkness |
| Und die andern sind im Licht | And others are in the light |
| Und man sieht die im Lichte | And one sees those in the light |
| Die im Dunklen sieht man nicht. | Those in the darkness one sees not. |

4. Busch, *Barth*, p. 473.

Finally there is the question of her legacy in the theological debate today, especially in two areas as controversial today as in the 1950s. The first is her understanding of the relationship of man and woman in the eternal order of things as well as in the contemporary world, and the second is the question of the ministry of women, including the ordination of women. Her views on the latter subject make her the unbeknown foremother of feminist theologians, and on the former the severest critic of many of them. Just as with Barth himself, she cannot be ignored.

Unfortunately it has not been possible for me to engage in much primary research into the life and work of von Kirschbaum because I have not been able to travel to Germany or Switzerland to study her letters or diaries, but have had to rely on the two works already noted, the standard biography of Barth by the young student who took over von Kirschbaum's work, Eberhard Busch, and Renate Köbler's *Shadow*. I have, however, subjected von Kirschbaum's own writings to close scrutiny, as well as the related passages in the *Church Dogmatics*, and spoken to a number of people who knew her, if not well, at least well enough to confirm or deny what is known about her from other sources.

Charlotte Emilie Henriette Eugenie von Kirschbaum was born on 24 June 1899 in Ingolstadt, Bavaria, because her father, Major General Maximilian von Kirschbaum, who was Bavarian, was stationed there. Despite her aristocratic name and lineage she grew up not in a castle or chateau but in her father's army residence. Her mother was Henriette, Freiin (Baroness) von Brück, whose family also rendered distinguished public service,[5]

---

5. The first Freiherr (Baron) von Brück, Karl Ludwig von Brück (1798-1860), presumably her grandfather, came from Elberfeld in the Prussian Rhineland. He was a successful businessman who founded the Austrian Lloyd and built up Trieste before taking service with the Imperial Civil Service and participating in the Parliament at Frankfurt in 1848. A brilliant career as imperial minister of commerce followed, when he successfully negotiated the customs union between Prussia and Austria. He wanted to see a "Greater Germany" of all nations and races. Falsely accused of financial corruption, he committed suicide.

and she had an elder brother, Max (b. 1897), and a younger brother, Hans (b. 1902). Significantly, the boys, as was customary in her class at this time, received a much better formal education than their gifted sister, but her father, recognizing her intelligence, encouraged her to read widely and well and took time to discuss what she read with her. Her mother, by now a semi-invalid and closer to her brothers, deeply resented this intimate relationship, and the two became progressively alienated until she and the surviving members of the family disowned the radical young intellectual on account of her friendship with a married man, Karl Barth.[6]

It is not clear whether von Kirschbaum was educated at home by the customary governesses or was sent to school, but the constant moves the family made as her father was transferred first to Munich, then to Ulm, followed by Amberg (Upper Palatinate) and back to Munich again meant that like so many army children, she could not put down roots anywhere. Inasmuch as she called anywhere "home," it was Munich, where she completed her secondary schooling in 1915 with a school-leaving certificate, not the *Abitur*, which would have entitled her to higher education. However, as Munich became increasingly identified with the National Socialist Party, and her friends, such as Georg Merz, the pastor who confirmed her, became increasingly right-wing, she distanced herself from "home." Such a peripatetic and precarious existence must have conditioned her outlook on life.

Nevertheless, it is interesting that despite nearly forty years' residence in Basel, she never applied for Swiss citizenship but retained German nationality to the end. Given her views on women's franchise, however, that might have more to do with

---

6. Köbler, *Schattenarbeit,* p. 38. Barth's family also objected, but did not actually sever the relationship (Busch, *Barth,* p. 185). Barth's deteriorating relationship with his younger brother Heinrich, who became professor of philosophy in Basel, was due to sibling rivalry and theological differences. Wolfgang von Kirschbaum later renewed contact with his aunt and acted as her executor.

the fact that German women had the vote, and Swiss women did not, than with any residual patriotism.

Her father's death in 1916, commanding the Sixth Bavarian Infantry Division in France, devastated her and reduced the family circumstances to such poverty that with the wartime shortages and price inflation she suffered malnutrition and permanent damage to her health. One day at the mother house of the Order of Deaconesses in Munich had convinced her that such a life was not for her. She was already earning a little money as an army censor, but now she left home and began her training as a Red Cross nurse.

Next to her father, the most important influence on the young woman struggling to survive in Munich during and after the Communist Uprising (1919) and the postwar economic collapse was undeniably Georg Merz, already mentioned as the Lutheran pastor who prepared her for confirmation, then as now a rite of passage in the Lutheran world, and for many the most important occasion in their lives for serious theological education. Encouraged by Merz, for whom she always retained a great affection, visiting him in 1957 when he was dying from the effects of multiple sclerosis, von Kirschbaum began reading voraciously, choosing contemporary theological works to assuage her hunger and grief. Her confidence was increased by the invitation to join the circle of intellectuals Merz had gathered around him, including Thomas Mann. She is remembered for the lively contributions she made to discussions on cultural, political, and theological topics. It was surely Merz who put into her hands a book by an unknown country pastor, Karl Barth, of Safenwil (Aargau). In 1919 Merz had "discovered" Barth's book in the course of his work as theological advisor to the publishing house Christian Kaiser Verlag of Munich and had struck up a friendship with the author, who felt that he had at last found someone "out there" who understood him.[7] The book was Barth's revolutionary *Rö-*

---

7. Köbler, *Schattenarbeit,* p. 22; Busch, *Barth,* pp. 112-13, 146.

*merbrief* (*Epistle to the Romans*, 6th ed., trans. E. C. Hoskyns [Oxford: Oxford University Press, 1933]).

One may also reasonably assume that von Kirschbaum eagerly devoured every volume of a new theological journal produced as the fruit of this friendship between Merz and Barth, *Zwischen den Zeiten*.[8] Begun in August 1922 on the basis of collaboration among Barth, Eduard Thurneysen, and Friedrich Gogarten, the journal continued until the end of 1933 when Barth and Thurneysen went into partnership with each other to produce the more radical *Theologische Existenz Heute*, and the others went their separate theological and political ways. In the 1920s Merz, now godfather to Barth's fourth child, Robert Matthias, was a regular visitor to the family; and on one occasion, because of her interest in dialectical theology, Merz took his protégée with him to hear Barth lecture. Barth then invited them both to spend a holiday during the summer of 1924 at his Swiss mountain retreat, the Bergli, outside Zurich. Her health shattered as a consequence of poor diet and the strenuous work and long hours of a nurse, she gratefully accepted.

The chalet to which Barth retreated was built by Rudolf and Gerty Pestalozzi in 1920. There they entertained a wide circle of friends throughout the year. Barth, who had been the first professor of Reformed theology at the University of Göttingen in 1921 and was called to a chair at Münster in 1925, was a permanent guest, with his close friends such as Thurneysen, and used the opportunity it afforded to recover from one term and prepare his lectures for the next.[9] Von Kirschbaum was gradually drawn into the center of this circle, becoming a close friend of Gerty Pestalozzi. When they got to know her better during her Bergli holiday in 1925, Thurneysen and the others convinced her that she

8. Köbler, *Schattenarbeit*, p. 23.
9. Eduard Thurneysen's father was a lifelong friend of Karl Barth's father, and his best man; Thurneysen and Barth were also lifelong friends, but had become particularly close when both were village pastors. See Busch, *Barth*, pp. 72-79, etc.

should have secretarial training. Ruedi Pestalozzi, a successful businessman, paid for this. When she completed the course she resigned her nursing post and spent a year as a welfare officer in the great Siemens company in Nuremburg. This experience of factory shop-floor problems helped to create her radical political stance so that during the war she would argue convincingly that one should work together with Socialists and Communists for common causes. She was never an ideologue for any party, however.

Since his wife Nelly was expecting a baby imminently and their house in Göttingen was proving difficult to sell, Barth moved to Münster alone, living in "digs" until he could buy a house large enough for five children. Another turning point in von Kirschbaum's life came when she visited him in February 1926, a month before the family arrived. It seems to have marked the beginning of her romantic involvement with him, and her commitment to do all she could to advance his work.[10] He began sending her manuscripts: a new edition of the *Römerbrief* to correct, a volume of his Göttingen lectures that he was about to publish, lectures on the Epistle to the Philippians,[11] and most important of all, a book published under the title *Die Lehre vom Worte Gottes: Prolegomena zur Christlichen Dogmatik* (Munich: Kaiser, 1927). This was Barth's first attempt at a project that resulted in the fourteen volumes of the *Church Dogmatics*. The first plan did not work to his satisfaction, and he laid it aside, but von Kirschbaum had caught the vision and would not let it rest.[12] To cut a long story short, when *Die Kirchliche Dogmatik*, volume I, part 1 *(Die Lehre vom Worte Gottes)*, appeared in 1932 as a result of her encouragement and hard work, the material was completely reorganized and a

---

10. Ibid., pp. 164-65; Köbler, *Schattenarbeit*, p. 29.
11. *Epistle to the Philippians*, trans. James W. Leitch (London: SCM, 1962). ET of *Erklärung des Philipperbriefes*, 6th ed. (Zurich: Evangelischer Verlag, 1947; 1st ed. 1927).
12. Busch, *Barth*, pp. 205, 211-15; Köbler, *Schattenarbeit*, pp. 42, 59-60.

subtle theological shift had taken place, as the changed title suggests. For from the outset von Kirschbaum was far more than a secretary and offered her criticisms and comments, even her advice as to whether something should be published.

She decided to go back to college again, this time in Berlin, where she now successfully took her *Abitur* and wrote a thesis. She also met Gertrud Staewen in 1928, who had been a friend of Barth since 1922 and was to be her own closest friend until her death.[13] Staewen recalled this meeting in a letter to Köbler:

> I see her before me now as she was in those early years when I first got to know her — it must have been around 1928 — and as she lives in my memory: dressed in fluttering pale blue silk clothes matching her lovely blue eyes, sensitive, delicate, but possessed by a scintillating, concentrated energy that was never loud but was always present. This energy, this zest for life, she had decided, entirely and completely, to exist only for one single human being, for his life, for his work, for his well-being and his peace of mind, for his friends and students.[14]

In April 1929 Barth began a sabbatical that lasted until the end of September, and he spent most of the time writing in the Bergli. It was also the beginning of his long partnership with von Kirschbaum, which lasted until von Kirschbaum's mind gave

13. Gertrud Staewen was one of Köbler's principal informants. She was a social worker in Berlin when Barth met her after giving a lecture there, and she became a regular guest at the Bergli. Her sister married another friend, Gustav Heinemann, a young lawyer and the future president of the Federal Republic. Staewen organized a scheme for helping Jewish refugees escape during the war, and after the war worked for the rehabilitation of prisoners and wrote several important studies. See G. Staewen to A. von Freudenberg, 7 Dec 1941, Inter-Church Aid files, WCC archives, Geneva. Quoted in Armin Boyens, *Kirchenkampf und Ökumene, 1939-1945: Darstellung und Dokumentation* (Munich: Kaiser, 1973), p. 326.

14. Köbler, *Schattenarbeit*, p. 32.

way and she became too ill to work any more, in 1964. They studied Luther and Augustine together, and she began her practice of reading books for him and preparing digests for him to include in his lectures, and above all in the *Church Dogmatics*. On 14 October 1929 she moved into the Barth family household and became part of it.

One should at this point interrupt the description of von Kirschbaum's life and attempt to describe her, if only to banish any suggestion that she was a poor, downtrodden, exploited secretary or that she was so lonely and fragile that she shamelessly used what assets she had, apart from good breeding, namely, exceptional intelligence and great natural beauty, to become a "kept woman." Barth probably acted with naive masculine logic and affection, because one wonders whether he really foresaw the consequences for his marriage or for her reputation. Nevertheless, he always took full responsibility for his decision, and for the subsequent predicament in which they found themselves.

The many snapshots taken during this period, particularly when they were at the Bergli, substantiate the testimonies of those who knew her. She was, by any standards, strikingly beautiful. Petite, dynamic, with luminous, penetrating blue eyes and raven black hair, usually twisted into a bun on the back of her head, but later on sometimes "permed," high cheek bones and slightly aquiline nose, she radiated joie de vivre and is most frequently caught in candid shots, laughing and sharing a joke with Thurneysen and other friends. There was an intensity, a charisma, and a warmth that was demonstrated also in her kindness to students, whom she was known to help out with books and a little money when they were in difficulty.[15] If she played "Mary" to Frau Barth's "Martha," one should not ignore the fact that she was a very efficient secretary. In fact, the first indication of her terminal illness was that during Barth's tour of America after his retirement in 1962, she started forgetting engagements, muddling up their

15. Ibid., p. 46.

10

travel arrangements, and failing to have important lectures ready on time. Until 1963 she traveled everywhere with Barth, both on family holidays and on lecture tours. There is even unsubstantiated gossip that the reason for his abrupt departure from the World Assembly of the World Council of Churches (WCC) in Amsterdam in 1948 was that he was irritated by the criticism of the degree of intimacy of their hotel arrangements. In fact, she was always at his side, ready with her typewriter day and night. She answered letters on his behalf, the Bonhoeffer correspondence in particular revealing her skills as a diplomat and mediator.[16] She took down his lectures from dictation and produced a perfect manuscript for him every morning; she checked and edited manuscripts for the press, chased references, produced précis of books for the card index, attended lectures given by Barth's opponents and produced summaries of them, and increasingly did much of the background research for his books as the years went on. Her hand is increasingly plain in the small-print sections in the *Church Dogmatics*. Like Victoria and Albert, she and Barth had adjoining desks. He dictated, she typed; she argued, he answered. It is reliably reported that in later years he would outline an idea and she would elaborate it and write it down.[17] It would be interesting to know who supplied the fine irony and the jokes in Barth's works, but clearly a strong sense of humor bound them together.

What bound all three together, Frau Barth included, was determination to see the *Church Dogmatics* completed. It is significant that when von Kirschbaum became incapacitated, the

16. Köbler, *Schattenarbeit*, p. 52; Eberhard Bethge, *Dietrich Bonhoeffer: A Biography* (New York: Harper & Row, 1970), p. 632 (February 1941, when Barth stood surety for him to the Swiss border control), p. 646 (autumn 1941; discussion of "Peace Aims"). Köbler places the incident in May 1942, when Bonhoeffer headed to Geneva, then cut short his visit to go to Sweden. It seems unlikely that he had time to visit Barth then. Busch gives the dates of his visits as 4 March, 31 August, and 19 September 1941. This is borne out by the documents quoted in Boyens, *Kirchenkampf und Ökumene*, 2:170-73.

17. H. Heck, assistant to Oscar Cullmann, Professor of New Testament at the University of Basel, told me this.

series came to an end, despite the efforts of Barth's new assistant, Eberhard Busch, and Frau Barth herself, who took over as much of von Kirschbaum's work as they could. Barth himself had already intimated that the final part, a theology of the Holy Spirit, should be written by the next generation of theologians, but, he said, "Lollo" (von Kirschbaum's pet name from childhood) would not hear of it.[18]

Several of those present on the occasion of the presentation of a *Festschrift* on his seventieth birthday in 1956 at the University of Basel have recounted to me the electric atmosphere when Barth entered leaning on the arms of his wife and von Kirschbaum, who were walking on either side of him. In the course of the ceremony he paid tribute to both of them, as well he might, because it is clear, from Busch's biography at least, that he would have achieved very little without either of them. The shock was created partly because for many years a discreet veil was drawn over von Kirschbaum's life by the Barth circle because of the "scandal" of her relationship with Barth.

There is no question that a divorce in prewar Basel would have ruined Barth's reputation and possibly his career, even if Frau Barth had agreed to a divorce. He, of course, had no grounds for divorcing the hard-working mother of his five children, a former member of his 1909 confirmation class in Geneva whom he had married in 1913 when she relinquished her ambitions to become a professional musician. The alleged adultery harmed von Kirschbaum most: even more than the disbelief among men that a secretary could become a theologian, it created

---

18. She wrote with regard to the completion of each chapter and volume: it was "always a breathtaking affair to see how such a chunk of rock evolved by almost imperceptible degrees through his constant concentration on innumerable and tireless efforts at chiselling and shaping." Letter to Helmut Gollwitzer, 19.10.52, quoted in Busch, *Barth*, p. 374. See also pp. 485-94. Barth was comforted by the fact that Mozart had been unable to finish the Requiem, and just as Sussmeyer had completed it he hoped one of the many students researching his theology would, but from the standpoint of pneumatology, not Christology. See Köbler, *Schattenarbeit*, p. 71.

the wall of silence around her name.[19] Rose Marie Barth, Barth's daughter-in-law, wrote: "Evil tongues in Basel, and especially elsewhere, found that the less they knew about the house in the Albanring, the more there was to talk about. None of them had any idea what suffering there was under the roof of this house. But the work of theology was happy . . . bound these three people together, held them above water, kept them from the brink of disaster."[20]

Thurneysen called the relationship a troika, something unique, which must be accepted as it was, but Busch writes of "unspeakably deep suffering" and tensions "which shook them to the core." So in the turbulent years of the German church struggle, the war, and its aftermath, there was also a struggle going on in the Barth family home, not least among the children, some of whom liked von Kirschbaum so much they called her "Auntie Lollo," while others took their mother's part and were estranged from their father.

It is important to understand that von Kirschbaum was not an employee but was treated as a family member. She was not only included on family holidays but was paid a monthly allowance, not a salary, which was held to be sufficient for her needs. She received no pension, but when she had to be hospitalized in 1965, the cost of the nursing home where she lived until her death in 1975 was met by the Barth family. She was buried in the Barth family grave with the agreement of Frau Barth, as Barth had wished, for he died first, in December 1968.

It is hard for professional women today not to feel outraged

---

19. Busch, *Barth,* pp. 59, 72-73, 185-86, 220; Nelly Hoffmann (1893-1976) was the daughter of Robert Hoffmann, lawyer and town clerk of St. Gallen (d. 1894), educated in Geneva because her widowed mother thought that the city offered the best opportunities to study languages and music.

20. Köbler was greatly assisted by Rose Marie Barth, a nurse studying theology, who married Markus Barth, Karl's eldest son, in 1940, having been counseled about the situation in 1938 by Thurneysen, who had confirmed her. See the prologue by Rose Marie Barth in Köbler, *Schattenarbeit.*

at the way Barth appeared to exploit both women, but neither saw it that way. Von Kirschbaum said in later years, "You know, he called me, and that was it," and almost her last intelligible comment to Barth after his weekly visit to her in the hospital was, "We did have some good times together, didn't we?"[21] She appeared to have no regrets, even though she walked a *via crucis*. She felt herself to be loved and cherished not only by Barth but by her many friends. What she herself gave in love and friendship is perhaps the inspiration for this moving passage in the *Church Dogmatics:*

> Love does not question; it gives an answer. Love does not think; it knows. Love does not hesitate; it acts. Love does not fall into raptures; it is ready to undertake responsibilities. Love puts behind it all the Ifs and Buts, all the conditions, reservations, obscurities and uncertainties that may arise between a man and a woman. Love is not only affinity and attraction; it is union. (III/4, p. 221)

Edwin Robertson got to know von Kirschbaum when he arranged for Kathleen Bliss to review the latest volume of the *Church Dogmatics* (III/3) for BBC Radio in 1950. He comments:

> There is no doubt that Charlotte was theologically necessary to Karl Barth, that without her he could not have done what he did. Her "subordination" [a reference to *CD*, III/4, p. 172, discussed below] was largely her choice because she recognised the great importance of Barth's work. Her own work apart from Barth lays the foundations for a feminist theology which goes far beyond the *Church Dogmatics*. . . . he is surely referring to her [when he writes] ". . . desiring nothing better than that this order should be in force, and realising

21. Busch, *Barth*, p. 473, quoting circular letter, May 1968.

Von Kirschbaum at age thirty, in
1929. She had begun working with
Barth several years earlier.

*Photo by Wolf von Kirschbaum,*
*courtesy of Pahl-Rugenstein Verlag*

Barth enjoying his pipe
*Courtesy of Pahl-Rugenstein Verlag*

Von Kirschbaum with Eduard Thurneysen
*Courtesy of Pahl-Rugenstein Verlag (Hans Prolingheuer)*

Von Kirschbaum with close friend Gertrud Staewen
*Courtesy of Pahl-Rugenstein Verlag (Hans Prolingheuer)*

Von Kirschbaum with Barth at the Bergli (above);
the two traveling together (below).

*Photos courtesy of Pahl-Rugenstein Verlag (Hans Prolingheuer)*

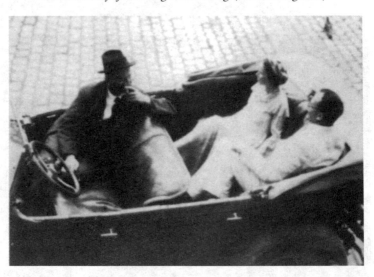

Von Kirschbaum and Barth, working side by side

*Top photo, Hans Prolingheuer; bottom photo,*
*Wolf von Kirschbaum.*
*Both photos courtesy of Pahl-Rugenstein Verlag*

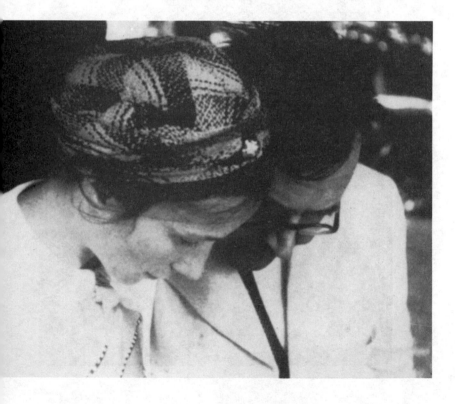

Von Kirschbaum shoulder to shoulder with Barth (above);
and working as a representative for the
"movement for a Free Germany" (below).

*Photos courtesy of Pahl-Rugenstein Verlag (Hans Prolingheuer)*

Von Kirschbaum is buried in the Barth family grave in
the Hörnli cemetery in Basel.

*Courtesy of Pahl-Rugenstein Verlag (Hans Prolingheuer)*

that her own independence, honour and dignity, her own special wishes and interests, are best secured within it. Thus in regard to the precedence which she sees man assume in this matter, she will feel no sense of inferiority nor impulse of jealousy. She will not consider herself to be attacked by this, but promoted and protected" [*CD*, III/4, p. 177]. This is one of the points in the *Church Dogmatics* where one would have liked to see a frank footnote by Charlotte![22]

It is Robertson's contention that the title of Köbler's book, *Schattenarbeit: Charlotte von Kirschbaum — Die Theologin an der Seite Karl Barths,* is mistaken, even though Köbler is careful to explain that *Schattenarbeit* means "shadow work" in the sense of the unseen, unpaid, unappreciated contribution that women make to the economy by their housework, child-minding, and upaid labor.

Robertson also said: "No one who visited Karl Barth at his home when Charlotte von Kirschbaum was intellectually active could possibly think of her as a shadow! She took part in theological debates and frequently was more prominent in the argument than Karl Barth himself. . . . I liked her and she was kind to me."[23] It is dangerous to see one text or one passage as offering a key to someone's life, but in the case of von Kirschbaum, the phrase at the end of Barth's tribute quoted at the beginning of this introduction, "I know what it really means to have a helper," is a vital clue since it is a deliberate echo of Gen 2:18, "It is not good that the man should be alone; I will make him a helper fit for him." This rendering, in the Revised Standard Version of the Bible, parallels Luther's translation, which uses *eine Gehilfin* for "helper." Barth and von Kirschbaum, however, quote from the Zurich Bible, which was used in Basel: "eine Gehilfe schaffen, die ihm ein Gegenüber sei." Both German

22. Edwin Robertson, private letter to K. D. Stoll, August 1990.
23. Robertson, letter to E. M. Jackson, October 1990.

23

translations use the word *Gegenüber* to describe their relation-ship. It is almost untranslatable, and in fact has been rendered in different ways in this translation of *Die wirkliche Frau*, but it can be rendered as "protagonist," "counterpart," even "sparring partner." Here it has the nuance of "sounding board," "part-ner," "other half." That was how von Kirschbaum herself saw her relationship to Barth, but also how she understood the basic relationship between men and women when it is not corrupted or debased by sin or sickness. This concept was fundamental to her theology as one can see from her writings in this volume, but here one must merely note that for her, a *Gegenüber* is also a counterweight — someone of equal strength and stature. Con-sequently, whatever the biological and psychological differences between man and woman, woman can never be considered in-ferior to man, because that would be a contradiction in terms, as well as a denial of God's creation. To return to Robertson, "There is a flash of understanding when male and female minds find a synchronicity. It can express itself in love, it can be sexual, but it is not always so."[24]

The nature of this relationship between two theologians has been discussed at such length because all theology is contextual, not just feminist theology, liberation theology, or black theology. This was their context; and for Frau Nelly Barth, Christian Socialist and former activist for social justice, Basel's narrow academic circles were equally oppressive.[25]

Not surprisingly, then, there is a scathing attack on the views of their erstwhile friend, Emil Brunner, for writing:

---

24. Ibid. He entitled the piece "Subordination as Mutual-Adaptation."
25. Barth himself was keenly aware of this. "It is good to think that the *Dogmatics* have emerged not only from my studies but also from a long and often difficult struggle with myself and with the problems of the world and of life. So if they are to be understood properly, they should be read not only with theoretical interest, but in an attempt to join me in the response to practical issues which has been my concern over all the past years." Letter dated 31 October 1963, quoted in Busch, *Barth*, p. 490.

The man is the one who produces, he is the leader; the woman is receptive, and she preserves life; it is the man's duty to shape the new. . . . The man must be objective and universalise, the woman must be subjective and individualise; the man must build, the woman adorns, the man must conquer, the woman must tend. . . . It is the duty of man to plan and to master, of the woman to understand and to unite. (*Man in Revolt*, trans. Olive Wyon [New York: Scribner's, 1939], p. 358; ET of *Die Mensch im Widerspruch*, 3rd ed. [Zurich: Zwingli, 1941], pp. 370-71)

There can be no "must" about it; and the stereotypes are objectionable and untrue to reality. To put the argument in a nutshell: "The divine command permits man and woman continually and particularly to discover their specific nature and to be faithful to it in this form which is true before God, without being enslaved to any preconceived opinions."[26]

It is important also to realize that von Kirschbaum was not in any way a "voice from the margins," but was at the heart of the Confessing Church struggle. She was elected to the parish church council in the fateful elections in 1933, typed the first draft of the Barmen Declaration on her typewriter (1934), and when she followed Barth into exile in Basel remained the confidante and supporter of Dietrich Bonhoeffer, Helmut Gollwitzer, Gertrud Staewen, and many others who remained behind. She was an independent participant in the studies commissioned for the Amsterdam World Assembly of the WCC and afterward. It is now known how unlikely it was that Hitler would invade Switzerland, but in Basel they were under constant threat and had to be prepared for evacuation at any time. They did not write with bombs dropping around them, as William Temple, William Paton, Donald and John Baillie, J. H. Oldham, and other leaders in the ecumeni-

26. *CD*, III/4, trans. A. T. Mackay et al., ed. G. W. Bromiley and T. F. Torrance (Edinburgh: T. & T. Clark, 1961), p. 153.

cal movement did, though they mourned the loss of William Elmslie and Fr. Tribe, collaborators on the British Faith and Order Commission killed by a "doodlebug" missile. Nor did they live in constant fear of the knock at the door, as French and German theologians did. Nonetheless, it was an insecure existence. This was especially the case when Barth won his campaign in 1942 to have Jewish refugees who were known to the WCC admitted to Switzerland. After the war, when Barth became fully, though critically, involved in the ecumenical movement, there were cold war tensions to deal with, so that the churches were not divided East and West as the countries of Europe and America were.[27]

To return to the narrative, in early 1930 Barth was invited to become professor of systematic theology in the Protestant Faculty of Theology in Bonn. He was 44, an age when many German theologians have already "arrived" and become largely set in their ways, as he humorously observed,[28] but for him it was a turning point. Faced with the need to revise the *Christliche Dogmatik* (1927) for his students, and confronted with the challenge of Anselm of Canterbury's *Cur Deus Homo?* which he and von Kirschbaum spent the summer studying, he altered his plans radically with the result that the first volume of the *Kirchliche Dogmatik* appeared in 1932, the same year that he welcomed the first English translation of the *Epistle to the Romans*.[29] This put the

27. Busch, *Barth*, pp. 303-15, 319, 322; Karl Barth, *An Open Letter from Switzerland to Great Britain* (London: Sheldon, 1941), banned in Switzerland. Barth had the distinction of being banned in Germany and Switzerland for advocating total resistance to Hitler. He made several BBC broadcasts. See W. Visser 't Hooft, *Memoirs* (London: SCM; Philadelphia: Westminster, 1972); Emile Fabre, *God's Underground C.I.M.A.D.E. 1939-45* (St. Louis, Mo.: Bethany, 1970); Karl Barth, *Against the Stream: Shorter Post-War Writings 1946-52*, trans. E. M. Delacour and Stanley Godman, ed. Ronald G. Smith (London: SCM, 1954).

28. Busch, *Barth*, p. 203.

29. Edwyn Hoskyns's translation effectively introduced Barth to the English-speaking world because it was the first of his major works (as opposed to monographs) to appear in English.

faculty "on the map," for although there had been eminent occupants of the chair before (most notably Albrecht Ritschl, 1846-64), for the first time the lecture halls were swamped with students, and Barth had to repeat his seminars several times a week, and allow larger numbers than he would have liked.

The family moved into lodgings in a stately residence on the south side of the town, and with them, of course, von Kirschbaum. Already a figure of some notoriety, Barth acted up to expectations by wearing to university functions the exotically colored cowl of an honorary doctorate of the University of Glasgow, bestowed on him on his first visit to Scotland in June 1931, for which both Barth and von Kirschbaum had studied English intensively. Von Kirschbaum was also learning Latin and Greek for the first time during the first years in Bonn. She was less successful in her attempts at mediation among those early advocates of dialectical theology, Brunner, Gogarten, and of course Barth himself. Barth was not unhappy to be involved in controversy as, urged on by questioning students, he was evolving the distinctive characteristics of his theology. At a lecture on "The Need of the Evangelical Church" in the packed new hall of the University of Berlin, fourteen hundred people cheered him to the rafters as he declared that the church needed to be unashamed of its gospel and recognize its need of it. "What the German people needs today is the existence of an *Evangelical* church, and not a *German* Evangelical church." He repeated the lecture to equally enthusiastic audiences in Bremen and Hamburg, laying the foundations of his reputation as a prophet with a new generation of students.

It was his students who protested when he was dismissed from his chair, on 26 November 1934, basically for refusing to start his lectures with "the German salute." Barth started his lectures with a prayer and maintained that his entire lecture was a prayer, so a political salute was inappropriate, but to no avail. He was the fourth member of the faculty to be dismissed for "political incorrectness," as their "crimes" would now be called, but the National

27

Council of Brethren of the Confessing Church, to which he had recently been elected, did not defend him, nor did any other church leader publicly, while he had made many enemies among the "liberal" theologians when he condemned them for accepting national socialist principles in the church. He was not offered any kind of position in the Confessing Church. Professors in Germany are tenured civil servants, and cannot lightly be dismissed, so Barth had to appear before a tribunal in Cologne to explain why he would not take the oath of loyalty to the Hitler government instituted in August 1934. Despite having a good attorney, Otto Bleibtreu of the Confessing Church of the Rhine, the dismissal was upheld. Barth had taken his stand, not on the Barmen Declaration, which he had written for the Confessing Church in their resistance to the German Christian Party's seizure of church government, but on Socrates' defense.[30] He argued that for the sake of his judges he must obey his God, rather than the state. Nevertheless, he felt somewhat vindicated when on appeal to Berlin the verdict was overturned, and he was merely fined for refusing to give the Hitler salute. The minister for cultural affairs then dismissed him under a notorious paragraph of the Law for the Reorganization of the Civil Service. That was Saturday 22 June 1935. The following Monday he was invited to take up a chair at the University of Basel. So although Barth was reluctant to leave Bonn and "the liveliest and richest days of my teaching life," since the Confessing Church had not offered him a teaching post of any kind, within a fortnight the family had moved to Basel and the house in the Albanring. No doubt they were helped by his eldest child, Franziska, who had married a Basel silk merchant in May 1935, an occasion when soundings about the appointment were made.

Von Kirschbaum, who had been the one to carry the notice to the Bonn lecture room announcing the cancellation of Barth's lectures and had conducted all the correspondence concerning the legal matters in Barth's dismissal, now took the courageous

---

30. Busch, *Barth*, p. 257.

step of "leaving her fatherland and friends" to go with him and carry on supporting him.[31] Her opposition had been more at the local level, where in some respects she could be more effective as a Lutheran church member than he, as a representative of the Reformed tradition. Where both of them parted company with many of the Confessing Church was in their unreserved and outspoken opposition to the Aryan paragraph, and their attempts to help those of Jewish descent or Jewish faith thus victimized. In August 1936 they traveled to Prague at the invitation of Josef Hromradka, who impressed Barth so much that he supported this ecumenical pioneer throughout his trials. However, the sight of the Jewish cemetery in Prague, evidence of the once flourishing community there, moved them most.

Von Kirschbaum wrote of the proceedings against Barth:

This event [the tribunal, etc.] is of profound significance and possibly even sets a precedent for the latest development of the Confessing Church. . . . We must indeed reconcile ourselves, Erica, to the fact that Karl's motives cannot be explained unequivocally to all people, perhaps only to a few. The many letters these days show us that some do grasp it. . . .

Yes, the path for the Confessing Church has now become very dark. The phony peace has already dawned. But, Erica, having our eyes opened this year has not been in vain. A fantastic letter from Niemöller [November 26, 1934] tells us that, too. The whole thing is now simply a revival of the *old* church, which, however, has no future in remaining as it is. We must have patience and be able to wait. I am sure that it is not the end. . . . It is very clear to me that Karl had to act in this way, and that comforts me whatever the consequences.[32]

31. Ibid., p. 262.
32. Köbler, *Schattenarbeit*, p. 48, quoting a letter to her friend, Erica Küppers.

One consequence was that she herself was in great danger when her passport expired in 1943. Without a valid passport she would be denied a Swiss residence permit and sent back to Germany. With great trepidation she handed her old passport in to the German consulate in Bern and it was promptly withdrawn. However, after representations she was issued a new passport the following day because the German vice-consul in Zurich, who was a member of the group conspiring to assassinate Hitler, took the matter in hand. That the danger was real can be seen from the fact that in October 1944 Elizabeth von Thadden, sister of the chairman of the Council of the Brethren, was summarily executed for corresponding in 1943 with Friedrich Siegmund-Schultze, a mutual friend and fellow exile.[33] Elizabeth von Thadden was betrayed by someone she trusted, as many were at that time. It is therefore not surprising that when Bonhoeffer appeared in Switzerland in March 1941 he was regarded with the utmost suspicion, since it was inconceivable to them how he could have got travel documents.[34] Bonhoeffer feared that Barth shared these apprehensions, and asked if he should, in the circumstances, cancel the much desired visit. It was von Kirschbaum who wrote by return mail to assure him of a warm welcome, though she also told him in no uncertain terms that Barth was mistrustful of any possible coup d'état by a group of Prussian generals, even though they knew Bonhoeffer was in some way involved. Barth reproached himself to the end of his days for insisting that Bonhoeffer's moral duty was to return to Germany (from the U.S.A. in 1939) in view of the consequences.[35]

33. Köbler, *Schattenarbeit*, p. 52. See Werner Hühne, *A Man to Be Reckoned with: The Story of Reinold von Thadden-Trieglaff*, trans. Robert W. Fenn (London: SCM, 1962), pp. 68-69.

34. See n. 16 above; Busch, *Barth*, p. 315; E. M. Jackson, *Red Tape and the Gospel: A Life of Dr. William Paton* (Birmingham: Selly Oak Colleges, 1980).

35. Busch, *Barth*, p. 315; Visser 't Hooft, *Memoirs*, p. 151; Eberhard Bethge, *Theologische Existenz Heute*, no. 214 (Munich: Kaiser, 1982).

The Swiss authorities reprobated any political activity by the many refugees and aliens within its borders, but became rather more tolerant when it began to become clear that the Allies would eventually win the war. In August 1943 in Zurich a group of German Communists who had been interned, together with various exiles and prisoners of war, formed the "Movement for a Free Germany." The title indicates their aims, and they created a committee to represent the different groups who had joined, and to direct the struggle against fascism and seek a free, independent Germany. They decided to have groups in each major city, and so formed one in Basel with Barth's support. In 1944 such activity was highly illegal. The representative of the Confessing Church in Switzerland was also working for the WCC, which precluded involvement in party politics. Von Kirschbaum was elected to replace him as its representative. She then became active in trying to hold the different parties in this alliance together, believing that all should work for the liberation of Germany and the creation of a just society. She found no difficulty in working together with Communists for this end and wrote pamphlets and made speeches to this end. She was much criticized for getting involved in politics at all, and for working with Communists, but she defended herself vigorously. The movement dissolved itself in December 1945, when it seemed redundant.[36]

Barth returned to Germany in August 1945 and met his surviving friends with joy. He got to know Martin Niemöller,

36. Köbler reproduced the program of "Free Germany" and a speech von Kirschbaum made in its support at St. Gallen, Geneva, and Montreux, July 1945 (*Schattenarbeit*, p. 77). Barth wrote that his house was almost like a branch office of the movement. "Lollo von Kirschbaum was active presiding over the matter with Langhoff and the former Prussian Secretary of State, Abegg." She got on extraordinarily well with "the red and reddish people" who were active in this group. Barth kept in the background, getting to know notable Communists for the first time. For his part, he brought them together with Protestant exiles. "Unfortunately the Christian exiles did not cut a very good figure alongside the much greater simplicity of the goodwill of the others." Correspondence quoted in Busch, *Barth,* pp. 324-25.

31

Bishop Wurm, and other leaders who had resisted Hitler whom he was prevented from meeting before. He had already been involved in the WCC planning for reconstruction in Germany and now was at the vital synod meetings that shaped the future of the Protestant churches in Germany, but missed the meeting in Stuttgart at which an unambiguous statement of guilt for the situation was promulgated. Ever the prophet rather than the politician, he thought Niemöller's wording too weak, but reconciliation with the member churches of the infant WCC was in large measure thereby effected.[37] However, his visit persuaded him to put the *Church Dogmatics* on the shelf for a year and accept an invitation to return to Bonn as a visiting professor. Von Kirschbaum accompanied him, and they found a tiny flat where they entertained many distinguished guests — celebrating Barth's birthday with potato salad, as there was nothing else to eat. The company made it taste better than the most sumptuous gateau. They got to know Konrad Adenauer but disliked him and were suspicious of his politics. When von Kirschbaum spilled a glass of red wine all over his trousers on one occasion at the Swiss consulate, it seemed symbolic![38] As British Council of Churches collaborators had managed to find themselves key British army and U.N. Relief and Rehabilitation Agency posts, Barth and von Kirschbaum were found passes so that Barth could lecture all over Germany, including Berlin. When he returned to Switzerland, his lectures were published, the new network of ecumenical friendships maintained, and every effort made to send practical relief in the shape of food, clothes, and books. Barth and von Kirschbaum spent the following summer semester (1947) in Bonn again, so it was not until late in 1948 that *Church Dogmatics,* III/2, the volume in

37. Busch, *Barth,* p. 329; R. C. D. Jasper, *George Bell, Bishop of Chichester* (London: Oxford University Press, 1967), pp. 295-96; Visser 't Hooft, *Memoirs,* pp. 191-94.
38. Busch, *Barth,* p. 333.

which von Kirschbaum's contribution first becomes clearly apparent, was published.[39]

*Die wirkliche Frau* was written in conjunction with ecumenical studies on the theme directed by Dr. Kathleen Bliss as part of a WCC study program. Dr. Bliss's book appeared in 1952 under the title *The Service and Status of Women in the Churches,* and is a good survey of the position of women and the opportunities open to them "to show what they could do," since they are the key people in the reconciliation of the church to the community that has rejected it as irrelevant. Von Kirschbaum had strong views on the ordination of women, as can be seen from chapter three and the appendix herein, "The Ministry of Women in the Proclamation of the Word (I and II)." In the appendix she quotes with approval the view of Canon R. W. Howard, an Anglican priest, but relates the question to her criticism of contemporary "monarchical" styles of Protestant worship and ministry that excluded laity of either sex from meaningful participation. Her thoughts anticipate ideas discussed in subsequent post-Evanston WCC studies on the laity and the church.[40]

If this is the immediate context of von Kirschbaum's writings, which represent also, as Busch shows, further development of what she had contributed to *Church Dogmatics,* III/2, the wider context was the influence of the "women's movement" upon her, on the one hand, and developments in Roman Catholic doctrine on the other. In one memorable incident when she and Barth had been to hear Hans Urs von Balthasar give a lecture

---

39. Completion was repeatedly delayed because of commitments to reconstruction in Germany, speaking tours, etc., though Barth was convinced that it was the most important contribution he could make to the postwar age. The volume concentrates on "The Creature": *mensch* — translated as "man," but every aspect of the human being in its theological significance is discussed. See Busch, *Barth,* p. 363.

40. See the bibliography in Harold Fey, ed., *A History of the Ecumenical Movement 1948-68* (Geneva: WCC, 1993), p. 501; H. R. Weber and S. C. Neill, *The Layman in Church History* (London: SCM, 1963).

in his controversial series, "Karl Barth and Catholicism" (winter semester, 1949-50), they all retired to Barth's favorite bar, the Charon, near the Spalentor, and Balthasar declared, "When I get to heaven, I shall go up to Mary, clap her on the shoulders, and say, 'Well done, sister!' " Von Kirschbaum immediately retorted, "And she will reply, 'Brother, you've got me wrong.' "

The appearance of Simone de Beauvoir's book *Le deuxième Sexe (The Second Sex)* provoked von Kirschbaum to attempt to develop a "Protestant doctrine of woman," since she had been in correspondence with de Beauvoir for some time and accepted much of her analysis of the situation, while criticizing aspects of her existentialist philosophy. Perhaps von Kirschbaum felt drawn to de Beauvoir because the latter's relationship with Jean-Paul Sartre was in some ways analogous to von Kirschbaum's own partnership with Barth. At any rate, while Barth wrestled with one of his most important ideas, "nothingness" (*das Nichtige,* which he used to illuminate the problem of evil), and experienced a breakdown of health so complete that he had to go to Locarno to recuperate, she went to Bièvres to deliver four lectures on the subject.[41] In the following spring, 1950, she went to Geneva and gave four lectures on de Beauvoir herself, then in early 1951 the Basel lecture translated here in the appendix, "The Ministry of Women in the Proclamation of the Word (II)."

She was nervous about giving the lectures, despite having made those speeches in wartime, so Barth gave her "ten rules for a speaker," summing up with "Don't be afraid; forget yourself, and remember that all will certainly be well." Since the lectures were published shortly afterward, presumably all was well.[42] (The significance of these lectures will be analyzed below.) She also

41. These lectures form chapters 1–4 of *Die wirkliche Frau.* See Busch, *Barth,* p. 363.
42. Busch, *Barth,* p. 363. *Die wirkliche Frau* was published by the Evangelischer Verlag, AG Zollikon-Zurich, who also published *Der Dienst der Frau in der Wortverkündigung* (The Ministry of Women in the Proclamation of the Word) in 1951. The latter is translated below in the appendix.

undertook a lecture tour of Germany in 1960. On 10 May 1956 Barth celebrated his seventieth birthday. In the midst of the family celebrations — Barth had the highest regard for his three daughters-in-law, one of whom von Kirschbaum had met in a lecture room and encouraged in her study of theology, and he had an especially close friendship with his son-in-law, Max Zellweger — and a private service of thanksgiving, the university feted him. At this function, he was presented with a *Festschrift* appropriately called *Antwort* (Answer).[43] Edited by their old friend Ernst Wolf, Rudolf Frey, and von Kirschbaum, who contributed a meticulous bibliography of 406 titles, it is an enormous tome of nearly a thousand pages, of weight commensurate with the *Church Dogmatics*. How catholic Barth's interests had become is reflected in the contributions from a Buddhist monk, analyzing his thought; a comparison between his theology and modern physics by a physicist friend; and an essay on Mozart, now an obsession with Barth. In the editors' foreword, however, there is almost as much written in tribute to their two close friends who had died after contributing much, Pierre Maury and Arthur Frey, as about Barth himself. Frey was the publisher of *Die wirkliche Frau*.[44]

When Barth's eightieth birthday was celebrated in 1966, with a slightly slimmer *Festschrift*, von Kirschbaum had already been committed to a nursing home for more than six months as her condition, first noticed during their tour of America on Barth's retirement in 1962, worsened. When she became aware in 1965 that her memory was going, she became acutely depressed. Barth himself in 1964-65 required several operations and suffered a stroke from which he recovered slowly. Preaching in Basel prison had been his joy on Sunday afternoons. Too feeble

---

43. *Antwort: Karl Barth zum 70. Geburtstag am 10 Mai, 1956* (Zollikon-Zurich: Evangelischer Verlag, 1956). See Busch, *Barth*, pp. 415-16.

44. Arthur Frey (1897-1955) was a close friend from Barth's first year back in Switzerland and courageously took over publishing the *Church Dogmatics* in 1937, when Chr. Kaiser of Munich was forbidden to continue doing so. See Busch, *Barth*, p. 285.

for that now, he visited von Kirschbaum and sang chorales with her. Both were nursed by Roman Catholic nuns, who obviously adored them and were clearly oblivious to their criticisms of Catholicism. Barth wrote in his final circular letter to his friends in May 1968 how much he looked forward to visiting von Kirschbaum, though she was only a shadow of her former self. "She's a great lesson to me in her frailty."

After Barth's sudden death one night in December 1968, Max Zellweger and other members of the Barth family visited her regularly. Her condition deteriorated as she regressed to childhood and lost the use of her faculties. She died peacefully on 25 July 1975. "It was a long, slow departure . . . she went farther and farther away."[45] The sermon at her funeral was given by an old friend, Helmut Gollwitzer, in the presence of many other friends from the Confessing Church struggle, including the then president of the Federal Republic of Germany, Gustav Heinemann. Gollwitzer gave thanks that she had accepted what in God's providence had been ordained for her, the joy and the pain and so many difficult tasks. Even her last ten years had been an example to them of forgiveness in Christ accepted.

There is an implication, made explicit in Köbler's *Schattenarbeit*,[46] that von Kirschbaum's fate was the consequence of the anguish and tension of her life with Barth. When her health broke down it was initially attributed to overwork, then was stated to be "brain disease," which could mean anything from mental breakdown to Parkinson's disease. Of course, if one designates her life as a *via crucis*, it is all too easy to see this dreadful end for an independent, intellectual woman as crucifixion. However, if one reads the description of the symptoms and

---

45. Hellmut Gollwitzer, "Predigt zur Beerdigung von Charlotte von Kirschbaum am 28 Juli 1975 — Friedhof am Hörnli, Basel," *Nachrufe*, no. 27 in the series *Kaiser Traktate*, p. 32 (quoted from Köbler, *Schattenarbeit*, p. 72).
46. Köbler, *Schattenarbeit*, p. 72.

the progression of the disease objectively, without any theological or moral judgment, it would appear to be Alzheimer's disease. So far research has only suggested that there might be a hereditary predisposition to it, and that water supplies contaminated with particular minerals might trigger it. There is no research in the public domain to suggest that it is stress related. Köbler also suggests that von Kirschbaum then similarly faded out of history, but in fact the year after her death Busch's biography appeared and gave her due credit. The question is not whether she is remembered or forgotten, but whether she is given the honor she deserves.

One can see from the above that it is difficult to separate the lives of Barth and von Kirschbaum, though one could argue that it was the change of work in 1930 that led to their mutual fulfillment, as much as the developing relationship. For lecturing in Bonn as professor in a rapidly expanding faculty stimulated Barth in a way that would not have happened had he remained in Münster, and being in Bonn meant a strategic base for both of them with regard to involvement in the Confessing Church struggle, while the move to Basel and subsequent work there was a challenge to be faced together. However, there is no doubt that, given that she was practically destitute and needed help even to acquire secretarial skills, it would have been difficult for von Kirschbaum to have become a theologian on her own. Her church, the Evangelical Lutheran Church of Bavaria, has only since 1975 begun ordaining women to the ministry, the last regional Lutheran Church in Germany to do so. How long Merz would have continued to help her as their theological and political convictions diverged in the 1930s is also open to question, while being a welfare officer in the Siemens company, Nuremberg, would hardly have engaged her intellect, though it increased her understanding of human relationships.

Von Kirschbaum herself would not have indulged in such speculation, since she saw her position as a calling, a vocation in terms of Luther's theology.[47] Later she understood her life's work in terms of Gen 2:18, as her man's helper, partner, companion, and counterpart, as her exegesis of the verse indicates. Nevertheless, her independence of character is clear throughout, while Barth was shaped into a civilized human being by Nelly Barth, who seems to have had more impact on his actual character, though there was always something about him of the Beethoven in the salons of Vienna, the same brusque grandeur.[48] It took all von Kirschbaum's diplomatic skills to keep the peace between Barth and his colleagues, but on occasion even she could not succeed.[49]

One of Barth's last books was entitled *The Humanity of God*, in which he was held to have mellowed his theology. One could also argue that his character mellowed considerably, though he retained his raucous sense of humor, his ability to shock, his prophetic powers, and above all his vision. He became more appreciative of his wife as a companion, envisaged idyllic retirement with her, and was grateful for her nursing skills. By contrast, von Kirschbaum seems to have become increasingly intense and vital, confident of her own abilities and determined to achieve her goals. In the period 1962-64 she underwent a crisis of faith and became depressed as she realized her illness meant she would not see the *Church Dogmatics* finished. As further decline set in, in 1965, she became more serene. It seems presumptuous to say this, but one is reminded of C. S. Lewis's wife in her final illness, and his comments about how her char-

---

47. See Gustav Wingren, *The Christian's Calling: Luther on Vocation* (Edinburgh: Oliver and Boyd, 1957).

48. "With its gentle pressure, marriage sets to work on so many of the bristly features which are man's by nature and helps to suppress them. . . . a wife gives loving criticism of sermons and speeches and is a spur to academic work; she is an extension of one's own work." Barth to W. Spoendlin, 20 June 1913, quoted in Busch, *Barth*, p. 72.

49. Busch, *Barth*, pp. 405-6: disagreements with Eugen Gerstenmaier, Hans von Campenhausen, Eberhard Müller; drifting away from the Pestalozzis.

acter was refined by suffering. One cannot estimate how much von Kirschbaum suffered as Barth's beloved, but one can appropriate the words Lewis imagines the Lord saying as he received Joy Davidman's soul — "A right Jerusalem blade." Only in her case, she was a tempered blade in her lifetime.[50] So just as it is almost impossible to disentangle her life from Barth's, so it is difficult to say what the real von Kirschbaum was like. It is a paradox worthy of Barth's theology that there are numerous descriptions of her personality, and there is the evidence of her letters and speeches, but despite her great capacity for friendship, there are hidden depths — her principles are clear enough, but what of her prayers?

I have devoted so much space to describing her life and relationships because her theology is so contextual. All theology is contextual, to use a cliché, but the writings in this volume relate particularly closely to a contemporary need: the need to understand and advance the position of women in postwar Europe. It is a sad reflection on the tenacity of the patriarchy that her theology has not reached its "expiration date" yet. Barth has often had labels attached to himself and his theology. Interestingly enough, it is difficult to do this to von Kirschbaum's writings, though one can see elements that are "Lutheran," "feminist," and so on. Just as there are Evangelicals, who have organizational coherence and a common theological framework sometimes elevated to manifesto status, and evangelicals, who are characterized by a concern for the gospel of a more generic but no less profound nature, so there are Feminists and feminists. Von Kirschbaum would not have identified herself with a movement or an ideological stance. She preferred to speak of women's duties rather than women's rights because of the emphasis she placed on a life of service and of

---

50. C. S. Lewis, *A Grief Observed* (New York: Seabury, 1961), p. 50. In 1968 Barth suffered severe depressions, which he seems to have overcome after emergency surgery on 21 August, the day the Russians invaded Czechoslovakia, an event that very much distressed him. See Busch, *Barth*, pp. 494-95.

partnership with the opposite sex. The quotation from R. W. Howard with which she concluded the Basel lecture is of the greatest significance. The argument therein runs to the effect that women will wear down the opposition by patient long-suffering and loving service until the quality of their ministry means that they cannot be denied any more. There is a Gandhian quality about this idea, but she advocates it on the basis of her exegesis of Pauline texts. Despite her unwillingness to identify with a movement, Edwin Robertson names her and Kathleen Bliss as the first feminist theologians he met.

Von Kirschbaum's work certainly displays several features associated with feminist theology. First, there is her careful, scholarly reexamination of the biblical texts, especially those used to justify the suppression of women, and her emphasis on the social context of the biblical writers. In her choice of texts and her exegesis there is an uncanny anticipation of present-day writers. Like many feminist writers she examines closely the archetypes of Eve, the mother of all living, and Mary, mother of the apostles, but she does not mince her words on the subject of Mariology. Second, there is the practical application of her theology, from the time of her first involvement in the Confessing Church struggle when she was elected to the church council in Bonn to her speeches in support of the Free Germany movement in Switzerland in 1944-45 and her exhortations to women to get involved in political questions. Third, there is the way in which she locates the relationship between man and woman in the divine order of creation, as a fundamental element in the relations between God and humankind, and as vital to the health of the church. Finally, perceiving an ambiguity in the position of Lutheran and Reformed churches on the subject of ordination, she pitches in with unequivocal arguments in favor of the ordination of women in 1951.

Examples of von Kirschbaum's careful treatment of biblical texts can be found throughout the present work. Many of them are familiar to us from later feminist works, but she, of course, cannot refer to their findings as a present-day writer would. There is, for example, her treatment of Ephesians 5 in the first lecture (pp. 54-68) or her even more painstaking analysis of what exactly is said about the women of significance in the New Testament in chapter two, "Women in the Life of the Church under the New Covenant."

However, her strength is in cross-referencing one passage to another and producing a composite picture of a concept such as marriage, or a person such as Mary the sister of Lazarus. It is typical that she concludes: "Thus all these incidents in which Jesus encounters women, as well as being personal encounters and ones that incorporate particular cases of practical help and support, are also symbolic representations of Jesus' encounter with his church."

She is concerned to draw out a pattern of the relationship that Jesus had with women, as well as to see types of Israel, of the church, and so on. Typology has always been a popular method and is seen in New Testament writers themselves. Is it a legitimate means of exegesis? The best example of this is her discussion of Eve, the "mother of all living," in chapter four below, as she seeks to uncover the biblical approach to motherhood.

She begins by contrasting Eve's position as Adam's partner and helper in Genesis 1 with the judgment pronounced on her in Gen 3:16, where only the fact that she will desire her husband indicates any independence on her part at all. Women had a disadvantageous position in later law, but women always reestablish their position through motherhood. What interests her is that the matriarchs (Sarah, Rebekah, Rachel, and Leah) bore children contrary to normal expectations, as bearers of the promise of the covenant, the hope of Israel, and it is the same with the mother of Samuel the prophet; with Ruth, ancestress of David; and with Bathsheba. "When faced with these stories, we are at a loss if we try to evaluate them as events occurring within the framework of purely human confusion and suffering. The golden thread running through them . . . is the line of descent . . . that culminates in the birth of *the* son." This is *Heilsgeschichte* pure and simple, taken for granted without any explanation, but

41

her conclusion is very important, namely, that a woman is a "mother of the living hope" through grace, not biology. In fact, from Isa 54:1, "Sing, O barren one who did not bear, . . ." she deduces that there is a form of motherhood that transcends the purely biological. Prophetic women can become spiritual mothers. She cites Deborah and Huldah before comparing this with the New Testament concept where motherhood is subsumed into the kingdom. Her treatment of the whole theme of motherhood, with its sublimation into a relationship to God's purpose and a means by which salvation is achieved, something that can be effected spiritually as well as physically, is clearly of great import for women who choose to follow their vision and pursue a career to the exclusion of biological children.

One of the most interesting sections of this book is the excursus, "Mary in Current Mariological Debate." Since the figure of Mary has become central to the feminist debate, it compels careful study. The style is rather clipped and dispassionate compared with elsewhere, reminiscent of similar passages in the *Church Dogmatics*, where the author sets out to survey all the available literature on the subject, rather than launch a scorching attack on some particular bête noire. Von Kirschbaum was writing before the promulgation of the encyclical *Munificentissimus Deus* (1 November 1950) when the centuries-old popular Catholic belief in the Assumption of the Virgin Mary into heaven was made official doctrine and Mary's secondary mediatory function was defined. Von Kirschbaum concentrates on the use of the term *coredemptrix* as a means of explaining the contemporary Catholic debate on the role of Mary in human salvation. The passage includes references to works in French, Dutch, English, and Latin as well as German, going back to 1901 in a comprehensive survey. Not surprisingly, she is interested in those theologians who see Mary as a helper for Christ, the new Adam, just as Eve was given to Adam, and in speculative interpretations of Gen 3:16 that both sexes participated in redemption just as they had in the Fall.

42

This coparticipation is based on the fact that it required Mary's willing cooperation for the Incarnation to take place, and now Mother and Son are so cojoined as to form one complete cause of salvation. Not only are her intercessions efficacious, but like Abraham she was prepared to sacrifice her son in perfect obedience. Von Kirschbaum also discusses the view of Scheeben that Christ poured his redemptive blood on humankind through his mother's heart, making her the channel of grace. "Through her collaboration in the redemptive sacrifice she helped win all salvation's graces; she became guardian of the whole merit of redemption for humanity; she is thus the true spiritual mother of all the redeemed and the ideal model for that church without which no one receives grace at all." Von Kirschbaum refutes these beliefs by quoting Catholic theologians such as M. J. Congar who oppose them. After all, 1 Tim 2:5 states categorically: "There is also one mediator between God and humankind, Christ Jesus, himself human." Also Mary herself was redeemed by Christ, and so could not have been actively involved in the work of salvation. Nor is there any question of her actions winning essential salvation through their merit.

Von Kirschbaum sees a dialectic here of two irreconcilable positions, but she dismisses the efforts of Dr. Heinrich Maria Koster to produce a synthesis that involves positing Mary as the pinnacle of humanity, a vital link between Jesus, who is both God and man, and the rest of humanity. His solution is, she says, to sacrifice theology for philosophy and to take refuge in Aristotelian-Thomist distinctions of form and matter. He blurs the distinction between the human and the divine; and yet, even though her sympathies as a Protestant are with the "opposition," she finds logic in the coredemptrix theses that is lost when theologians attempt both to appeal to Scripture and to submit their formulations to the teaching office of the church as the ultimate judge of the correctness of doctrine.

Unlike many theologians, however, she recognizes that what will be determinative in the eventual Mariological formulation will

43

be popular liturgy and belief, which have long since overtaken the theologians. Yet since the Roman Catholic Church is never exclusive in its thinking, there will be no resignations. The whole debate is simply evidence, it seems, that human frailty is such that one must seek further solace in Mary. Von Kirschbaum's own thoughts are found in chapter four below, preceding the excursus.

In the context of a discussion of the roles of prominent women in the Hebrew Scriptures, who are justified not by biological motherhood but by whether they fostered hope and strengthened the covenant relationship between God and his people, she turns to Mary, "an undistinguished virgin." She expounds the significance of the Annunciation (Luke 1:38) as a response of faith, quoting Luther, "For she was flesh and blood as we are. That is why she had to let go of everything, including herself, and cling only to the word which the angel proclaimed from God" (Weimarer Ausgabe, 17/II:399). She sees in the meeting of Mary and Elizabeth the first manifestation of the church of the new covenant, an original idea, poignant if only it were not an anachronistic use of the concept of "church."

She delights in contrasting Mary's dire predicament as an unmarried mother under the law with the grace of God as the Holy Spirit creates a child within her. "So defenseless and vulnerable is the entry of the eternal son into this world that a simple craftsman has to help in order for his simplest conditions of existence to be met." However, her conclusion is even more striking: "Even if history should ascribe the historical event to a man, the story of Jesus Christ is not a story of men. Men are conspicuous by their absence at the birth of the Lord. Mary is a *virgin* mother." The reason for this, she concludes, is so that Jesus' birth would be a miracle of grace, not the product of human agency. God acts alone, and it is intended that the sign of the virgin birth should reverse the judgment on women in Gen 3:16, "And he shall be your lord" (here she quotes *CD*, I/2, p. 212). In view of what von Kirschbaum writes elsewhere about the partnership of the sexes, however, it is unlikely that

44

she intended by these words any support for mothers single by intent. She goes on to see in the words of Jesus on the cross entrusting his mother to his disciple (John 19:26-27) the establishment of the path for Israel (of which Mary is the representative) into the apostolic church. Mary's role is thus strictly limited, namely, to draw Israel into the church. "Whoever claims more than this deviates from the gospel," she states dogmatically.

Since Mark's Gospel states explicitly that the women were "at a distance" from the cross (Mark 15:41), it is difficult to see any historical basis for this incident, however satisfying it may be theologically. Such considerations do not worry her here, but she applies historical-critical methods to reject subsequent traditions about Mary's "immaculate conception" and "assumption into heaven." Ultimately she aligns herself with Luther in seeing the story of the Virgin as encouraging the poor and lowly to understand that they too will be recipients of grace, and in denouncing the elevation of Mary above other mortals as idolatry.

*Die wirkliche Frau* continues with an extended discussion of her friend Gertrud von Le Fort's book *Die ewige Frau* (The Eternal Woman), which contains a description of Mary as virgin, bride, and mother. The crucial question, though, is whether a woman can be the vehicle of divine revelation, or whether in popular devotion Mary has not become confused with the content of the revelation itself, and what the implications are for ordinary women. For Le Fort, "the salvation of the world is tied up with the restoration of the image of Eternal Woman by women, and its revitalization for the world." Mary has become a symbol that represents the eternal truth about humanity. Women should emulate her, but men may also reflect this eternal image. Thus, von Kirschbaum concludes, the Mary of Catholic Mariology, the Queen of Heaven, is "the bold dream of the exaltation and glorification of creatures endowed with grace."

She contrasts this "Marian anthropology" with the New Testament teaching that Jesus Christ is the perfect image of God, and outlines an anthropology based on Christology. Mary is a myth, devotion to which obscures reality for the believer. Indeed, following the ideal she represents makes people profoundly solitary, whereas man and woman were made for one another, and in each individual human being the masculine and the feminine must be held in complementarity.

She therefore passes to a critique of Simone de Beauvoir's book *Le deuxième Sexe (The Second Sex)*, which had just been published, and concerning which she corresponded with the author and gave lectures. In a nutshell, she applauds de Beauvoir's analysis of the social relationships between men and women, the description of the oppression of women, and her outline of the image of woman in literature. However, she rejects the "existentialist morality" and the concept of freedom that inform de Beauvoir's views. Von Kirschbaum does see parallels between the existentialist demand and the biblical call to follow Christ, and thinks Christians and existentialists can walk some way together. But true liberation consists of appreciating the complementarity of the sexes in God, not in standing in isolation without God. When men and women bear witness to the truth of their existence there will be no possibility of "inauthentic domination and subjection."

These beliefs stem from her thesis that men and women have meaningful existence only as they stand together in the primal relationship of the Genesis story (Gen 2:23). Man and woman are as they are because of the way they were defined by God in creation, so the relationship goes to the foundation of the world. They realize their human potential as they fulfill the covenant demands. Gender is of the essence of humanity, not its incidence, so redemption is achieved as man, as woman. Many feminists would not agree.

One could write another chapter discussing this point, but the implications are obvious. It is better to read her arguments and evaluate them oneself. Her standpoint on ethical and political issues has already been sufficiently described above in the biographical treatment of the development of her theology.

As von Kirschbaum notes, where ministry is a congregational and corporate responsibility, as among Congregationalists and Quakers, there is no difficulty about integrating the ministry of women, and women enjoy complete equality. At the other extreme, churches in the Anglican communion are engaged in a heated debate about the position of women. In 1951 there was great diversity of practice among them, but agreement that women could not be ordained. Today most Anglican churches allow the ordination of women, but the debate continues.

In her discussion of the ministry and ordination of women as found in the appendix, "The Ministry of Women in the Proclamation of the Word (II)," von Kirschbaum reduces the issue to two succinct questions:

> *Does the New Testament contain an authoritative concept of office that by its very nature excludes participation by women?*

and

> *Does the Pauline reference to women's position of subjection bar them from participation in the ministry of the proclamation of the Word?*

To answer the first question she turns to the Old Testament tradition of a male priesthood with its exclusive rights of access to God in the innermost sanctum of the temple in Jerusalem, and its duty of mediation between God and humanity. She attributes the Roman Catholic resistance to the ordination of women to the continuation of this system implied in the Catholic claim that Mass is a bloodless repetition of Christ's sacrifice on Golgotha. In the New Testament Jesus' death is the sacrifice that ends the system, while he is the mediator who enables the entire community to have direct access to God. For her the doctrine of the priesthood of all believers means precisely that, women as well as men being included. But priesthood means service. Therefore, "all human actions can henceforth only be forms of service to the actions of the Lord himself." They must imitate Christ in

47

being the servants of all and embracing the suffering this involves. Those who follow this path are the communion of saints, serving Christ by serving each other. All have need of each other and all receive spiritual gifts without distinction with regard to their sex (Acts 2:17). It is on the basis of her perception of the biblical nature of Christian ministry that von Kirschbaum builds her case.

Like many feminist theologians after her, she sees great significance in the fact that women were the first to see the risen Lord and that they were sent by him to the disciples, but she does not see this commission as in any way commensurate with the apostolic commission, bestowed exclusively on men, endowed with the Holy Spirit (John 20:21-22), through whom the church was called into being. The church as a whole is invested with authority to proclaim the Word of God and to commission individuals to this task and other acts of service, but this can be done only by recognizing the God-given gifts of individuals in obedience to its Lord. This acknowledgment of the corporate responsibility of the church places constraints on the charismatic freedom of individuals and makes possible the evolution of temporary systems of church order "until the kingdom comes." She does not see any conflict between a Pauline charismatic ministry and a church continuing Jewish traditions simply because the new community represented a radical break with past structures. There are no offices in the earliest church per se, only forms of service, and no distinction made between clergy and laity. On this basis, the ministry of women cannot be excluded as contrary to divine command, and she rejects the arguments of those who distort the sense of Reformation statements of faith to assert that they are excluded. Authority comes through the ministry of the Word, which can be exercised only by constantly renewed grace and by the Spirit, not because of the inherent nature of one's office. The answer to the first question is therefore negative.

Her answer to the second question rests on a detailed analysis of 1 Corinthians 12–14, which she sets firmly in the context of the wider themes of the epistle. She is vehemently opposed to the practice of taking verses or even chapters in isolation, demonstrating that in the case of this passage, the restrictions on women can be understood as totally prohibitive if taken out of context. A completely different positive interpretation emerges if the letter is taken as a whole.

Equally she castigates women, such as the novelist Pearl Buck, who reject Paul on the basis of a few unpalatable verses taken out of context. It is not Paul who is at fault but his interpreters who use such verses as a "police warning," she says; but Paul has notwithstanding been labeled a misogynist by succeeding generations of women.

First Corinthians 12–14 are about the relationship of charisma and ministry, which are in conflict in the congregation in Corinth. "The church will be built up only through the knowledge that is rooted in love, and therefore only through the charisma that, instead of being self-serving, is put into the service of the Lord and his church." This is the core of Paul's argument. Of course Paul acknowledges that women receive the gifts of the Spirit as well as men, but von Kirschbaum believes that what he writes here and in the famous passage requiring women to veil their heads when they prophesy (1 Cor 11:5) indicates that women minister as women, and gender differences are not obliterated by charisma (pace Gal 3:28). Men and women are absorbed equally into the unity of the children of God and as children of God have special responsibilities according to their gender. It is stated, she says, that "the man is the head of the woman" (in 1 Cor 11:3) because that is the order in which men and women are placed in partnership, giving the man the leading role. While women should acknowledge their place in this partnership, it does not mean that they are in any way inferior, or that this verse is simply to be taken as evidence that Paul was conforming to the norms of his age. For in the wider context of Paul's thought, it is clear that women are in no way inferior to men. Just as Christ is Lord of all and the servant of all, subservient in all things to his Father's will, so men and women are both, in their respective positions, directly subordinate to Christ.

She quotes Luther with approval, that each and every kind of thing is what it is because God created it so. "The fact of my being a man or a woman is part of the uniqueness of my existence that has been determined by the will of the Creator." So to deny one's femininity is to deny God's design.

It is clear from her argument that von Kirschbaum would not approve of today's clergywomen in their cassocks and clerical collars aping male behavior patterns, because for her it would be essential to the ministry of women that new feminine models of ordained ministry be created under the Word of God. Both sexes are under an obligation to complement each other in their ministry. For her, man is called "the head" simply because he was called ahead of woman and given responsibility to preserve the balanced relationship. Woman is called to assist, to be his counterpart, and his existence is unthinkable without her. The complementarity of their relationship is fulfilled in the relationship of Jesus Christ to his church (Eph 5:22) so that they may live together as people who have encountered each other in this way "from the beginning." This is the proper relationship in Christ, and any attempt by the man to dominate on the basis of Gen 3:16 is an attempt to revive the old order of the former covenant, destroyed by sin, and replaced by the new covenant in Christ. (One should note that throughout her exegesis, von Kirschbaum pays minimal attention to questions of authorship. That Ephesians is not written by the author of 1 Corinthians and can be dated to about AD 90 is not a problem for her. We are left to infer from her grammar that she does not consider 1 Timothy to be Pauline.)

These ideas are developed more fully in the *Church Dogmatics* (III/4, pp. 171-80). They are crucial to understanding her concept of ministry. If one cannot appreciate this "great mystery" (Eph 5:32), one cannot understand the position of women and their responsibility that correspond to Christ's. The church needs

50

women because their humility and their "silence" as "pupils in the school of God" (Calvin) are reminders of what the church should be and the "subjection" it should embrace. A listening church is needed as much as a teaching church. The question, however, is whether this "subjection" debars women from participating in the ministry of the Word. The problem is that the term *hypotagē,* "subjection," has become overlaid with cultural and theological preconceptions that conflict with the original meaning and that are used to justify either outraged rejection of an unreasonable demand or "clueless, . . . ripely bourgeois, indolence." (Given von Kirschbaum's known political sympathies, it is not surprising that mindless conformism is for her the greater sin.) These views arise from the mistaken attempt to dismiss the God-given gender difference and the mutual complementarity intended from the beginning of creation as a situation to be transcended. Indeed, a woman should accept her place without making invidious comparisons; she should rejoice in her femininity, secure in the knowledge that she is in no way inferior. The point is that this should be a free choice, made in response to her perception of God's command, not something imposed on her. How she interprets her responsibility for mutual complementarity will be her decision.

For whereas congregational worship was once so chaotic that restraint and order were the command of the apostle, today the reverse applies. Not only women are silent but whole congregations. One highly educated, theologically trained man monopolizes the conduct of worship while the congregation sits slumped in almost total passivity. *Stumme* is her wonderfully evocative word. She pleads vehemently for a change in church order to allow the Holy Spirit in. Women are urgently needed to speak out now, not to keep silence, and recall people to a New Testament model of service, thus building up the church in apostolic fashion. Women should become active preachers of the Word only if they feel they have a call to do so, but they should have no doubts about the legitimacy of their ordination. By their very nature they are unlikely to lay claim to God's authority. One

51

may anticipate, too, that women will develop other forms of ministry besides the overly dominant preaching ministry (of the Reformation tradition). Indeed, women should not sit around waiting for an opportune moment for ordination, but should work out their own way forward with their eyes fixed on a responsibility that will not be gainsaid. The problem is that although this argument provides a means of reconciling two apparently contradictory passages in 1 Corinthians (11:3-15; 14:3-36) by use of Ephesians 5 and by an appeal to the eternal order of things created by God and reaffirmed in the relationship of Christ with his body, the church, it depends on one accepting the allegorical interpretation of the Hebrew Scriptures in Ephesians 5 and the mutual complementarity of the sexes as existing "from the beginning" in the framework of Luther's doctrine of the orders of creation. Difficulties arise if one emphasizes the common nature of all humankind (Acts 17:26-27) rather than their distinctiveness. Nevertheless, she is right to assert that women do, by nature of their history, have a special responsibility for church reform and a rediscovery of charismatic ministry, and her description of how they should achieve ordained status is in many ways prophetic. There must be a sound theological base for the ministry of women, whether ordained or not, so that they may act with confidence and not have to rely on arguments from precedent or the secular context.

There is much more that one could write about von Kirschbaum's theology, but it is better to let her speak for herself. It is a theology of mutual complementarity: complementing not just Barth's theology or Luther's sermons, but the experience of readers themselves.

# FOREWORD

THE following work originated from four lectures on the biblical witness about woman, which I gave in Bièvres, France, this year and which I have revised in response to the wishes expressed for their publication. The work is a sketch and no more. If, in spite of that, I am publishing the lectures, it is because I hope that even in this modest form the work can be of definite service.

An attempt has been made in chapter five to create a distinction between a Catholic Doctrine of Woman, as Gertrud von Le Fort calls it, and existentialist philosophy's concept, as it is found in the recently published first part of Simone de Beauvoir's book *The Second Sex*. Neither path is ours.

Our path, namely, the search for a Protestant Doctrine of Woman, is the concern of this book. May others, who can do it better, take up this concern of ours and continue the quest.

Charlotte von Kirschbaum
Basel, September 1949

## ❖ 1 ❖

# JESUS CHRIST AND THE CHURCH — MEN AND WOMEN

THE "question of woman" is older than the so-called women's movement, which began to emerge around the middle of the last century and whose earliest phases — even though its aims and motives were different — ran parallel to those of the workers' movement. In both cases it was the changed economic situation that created new conditions of existence for workers and women alike.

The "question of woman" is linked only secondarily to these new conditions of existence, for the question it raises is that of the nature of women's existence as such, of what it really means to be a woman. Nowadays people are inclined to reject this question as unnecessary and based on a misunderstanding, detecting here an accommodation to the myth that *le male* has invented for himself. If there is no "question of man" why should there be a "question of woman"? Are women perhaps not equally human beings just like men? Of course they are. Humankind exists as male and female and only in the unity of this twofold nature. A human being taken on its own in isolation is not a real human being, but an abstraction in human thought. The real human being exists as a man alongside a woman, a woman alongside a man. There is no such thing as a woman existing in isolation any more than there is such a thing as a man existing in isolation. For precisely this reason, however, a specific question

55

about woman arises, because she, by her very nature, poses in a particularly acute way the question of what the humanity of human beings consists in, of what distinguishes human beings from other creatures.

The biblical creation narrative tells in the form of a myth or legend how God created human beings as the final act in his work of creation, and how he introduced this act with the words "Let us make humankind in our image, according to our likeness" (Gen 1:26). (For this whole section see Karl Barth, *Church Dogmatics* [hereafter *CD*], III/1, §41, pp. 191ff.)[1] Thus the biblical witness envisages God, before he proceeded to act, engaged in a debate with himself, in an internal encounter. According to this idea of his, God himself is not solitary, but exists in relationship despite his unity and unique quality. And it is clearly an important part of this biblical testimony that this should be expressed prior to reporting the creation of humankind. "So God created humankind in his image, in the image of God he created them; male and female he created them" (1:27). That is the basic form in which humankind exists: the differentiated duality of male and female. Thus God created not a solitary human being but human beings in relationship, that is, in a manner corresponding to his own nonsolitariness. He placed human beings in a mode of existence similar to his own. Existing then as male and female together, human beings are made in the image of God.

If one looks for *this* human quality of being made in the image of God in *that* similarity, and not in some attribute of the individual person, then it becomes immediately apparent that being made in his image is neither a quality inherent in humanity nor a human achievement but rather is precisely the fact of having been created in this differentiated duality, in the man-woman relationship. From the moment of creation onward

1. For further development of the argument, see *CD*, III/4, §54, pp. 116ff. — Ed.

God placed humankind in this situation of encounter, so that humankind does not exist in solitariness — on the contrary, humankind exists in the form of man (and therefore in relationship with woman) and the form of woman (and therefore in relationship with man). In this differentiated duality, man and woman together constitute the humanity created by God and chosen by him to be his counterpart in creation. It is this humanity that God seeks to engage in intimate mutual I-Thou encounter. Without the human race the rest of creation would be merely an entity different from God. It is not in its own intrinsic nature created for such an encounter. The creature that God has chosen and determined for this encounter is humankind, and precisely in its dual form as man and woman at that. Since human encounter is constitutive of its very being, by the same token humanity is ready for encounter with the divine, that is, for divine grace. The relationship between the sexes derives its central position from this, and what distinguishes it from sexual differentiation among animals is that the differentiation between man and woman is their only differentiation, and the one underlying everything else that has to be said about humanity. Being man or woman will be a factor in everything that human beings are and do, and therefore it is imbued in every respect with this basic form of human community. Thus the characteristics of being creatures and part of nature, which humans share with animals, are not something "animal" but something specifically human, and that is so because it pleased God to make the human life-form correspond to his own divine life-form.

The second creation narrative (Gen 2:18ff.) gives basically the same account of the creation of humankind but is far more detailed and colorful when it comes to depict the creation of woman — and only at that point, of course, is the process of creating humanity completed, for only a humanity containing woman is the humanity with which God is well pleased. "It is not good that the man should be alone. I will make him a helper as his partner" (v. 18).[2] The lonely individual needs a "helper" [or partner] in order to avoid being lonely any longer. He is unable to help himself, to overcome his loneliness through his own resources. God has to offer him this "helper." He cannot find it elsewhere in creation, for even though he can name the animals, thereby determining their nature, this does not make them intimate companions — they remain part of his surroundings. The individual remains lonely, therefore, unwilling to exchange his loneliness for a false companionship.

A shared existence emerges for the first time with the appearance of woman. She complements him as his "helper." It is with her that the fellow human being appears on the stage, with all the promise that this appearance entails, but also demands, thus limiting any notion of self-sufficiency. The "I" is faced with a "Thou," and is in turn challenged as "Thou" by the other "I." This does not happen without suffering, that is, without an assault on, a clutching at, the lonely individual. What is symbolized here in the myth is the way in which God both needs and uses people themselves in order to help them. He inflicts a potentially fatal wound, removes a rib, and from this makes woman. While this is happening Adam lies in a deep sleep and is thus only a passive participant: the "helper" is not his doing. He does not awaken until she is already standing there before him, a human being like himself, but not himself, a human being with all the alienness of another human, in whom he recognizes himself, not as a replica of himself, but as a mysterious yet infinitely intimate "other," someone whom he can recognize only as a "helper" God brought to him, whom he cannot continue to view as an object in his surroundings, whom he can encounter only as a "Thou," as a fellow human being in the closest, most intimate, form. This is what woman means for man.

2. NRSV here is close to the Zurich Bible, which von Kirschbaum used and which differs significantly from the Luther Bible at this point. Literally translated it reads: "a helper who will be his counterpart," or perhaps, "will complement him." — Ed.

And man "recognizes" her: "This at last is bone of my bones and flesh of my flesh." And he names her, thereby naming himself for the first time too: "this one shall be called Woman [*ishshah*], for out of Man [*ish*] this one was taken" (v. 23). In the encounter with woman he becomes man.

Man's affirmation of woman is a human decision permitted by God in freedom. It must not fail. For God does not want to impose it as a fate hanging over him ("like a bolt out of the blue signaling the splendor of paradise and the dignity of man made in the image of God," as Ph. Theodor Culmann puts it in *Die christliche Ethik* [Kaiserlautern: 1863], where he already detects the beginning of the Fall in the creation of woman!). Instead he offers it as a sign of grace, to be recognized and affirmed as such by humans.

And so man and woman face each other in an ultimate freedom, and in an ultimate bond: in an ultimate freedom, because each of them has emerged from the hand of God, and in an ultimate bond because it is both together who constitute the humanity in whom God is well pleased, and whom he has chosen to be his creaturely "Thou." That is the ultimate, deepest form of equality between man and woman — rooted more in equal grace and redemption than in equal rights.

The realization of this unity can occur only as man fully makes the recognition and affirmation implicit in the words: "Therefore a man leaves his father and his mother and clings to his wife, and they become one flesh" (v. 24). What emerges here is the marriage bond based on love. Man will renounce all previous ties for the sake of this one necessary tie, and allow his real unity with woman to find fulfillment in complete union. "And the man and his wife were both naked, and were not ashamed" (v. 25). If the union of man and woman is the expression of their real unity, no sense of shame will be possible, for man will recognize the woman as his wife, and woman will recognize in man her husband. A sense of shame can appear only where man or woman imposes male or female reservations, where their union does not bring about the realization of their unity, where companionship has long since secretly turned into opposition, a possibility envisaged in the creation of humanity but made real through their sins.

When humans destroyed their relationship with their divine companion, in wanting to be like God, by the same token they destroyed their human companionship; Genesis 3 tells the story of their fall. The biblical account — which, we are not too quick to say, was told of course by a man — has woman appear as the one who speaks and acts first. Companionship as such is not dissolved completely — humans necessarily retain the characteristic of being made in the image of God — but it gets distorted almost beyond recognition: man's "helper" assists him to sin. That is why man accuses woman, when God calls him to account: "The woman whom you gave to be with me, she gave me fruit from the tree, and I ate" (v. 12), and why God begins his pronouncement of judgment on man with the words: "Because you have listened to the voice of your wife . . ." (v. 17). Woman's role is presented in the Bible as being as pivotal as that: created by God to be, through her very existence and through her entry into the life of man, the "helper" man needs in order to become, together with her, God's creaturely companion, she "helps" him to destroy the companionship with God and with it the companionship between man and woman. "I will greatly increase your pangs in childbearing: in pain you shall bring forth children" (v. 16) — this is the judgment that then falls on woman.

The man who wrote this text was an Israelite. He had the historical reality of his people in mind, and hence too the suffering incurred by his people as a result of their failures, the judgment through which God always had to punish their unfaithfulness to him. Israel breaks the covenant made by God with the forefathers, showing itself to be an unworthy partner. Yet God sticks to his promise and does not reject his people. And so one finds in the books of the prophets alongside the words of judgment, in which Yahweh appears as the husband of adulterous

Israel, words of hope and promise also. The Old Testament knows of a fulfillment, of a "betrothal in righteousness, loving-kindness, and mercy." Israel is nourished by hope in the Messiah, the one who will save his people.

Thus the Israelite author perceives the man-woman relationship as in essence destroyed, no longer capable of fulfillment, lacking the capacity for fulfillment from within its own resources, but dependent on hope in a future eventuality. He sees man and woman basically as oriented toward their progeny. Adam, expelled from paradise, does not greet his wife with the words "This at last," and he no longer calls her "Ishshah," but "Eve," "mother of all living" (3:20). She may now be his "helper," in as much as being mother of his children she becomes for him bearer of hope. For the sake of a future son, the man now seeks a wife, and for the sake of protecting his seed he circumscribes marriage with the strictest of laws and punishes adultery with death. He is now truly the woman's master, and no longer "her husband" and the object of her desire.

All the more astonishing, then, that there should resound in the middle of the Old Testament the Song of Songs, the Song of Solomon, exulting in the covenant between man and woman and singing the praises of the unquenchable longing and the unconditional union of the lovers. The encounter of man and woman described in Gen 2:18-19, the fulfillment of their counterpoised "I" and "Thou," reappears here as the dominant theme, only now it is above all the voice of woman that is also to be heard. What seems to emerge in the eschatological context of this depiction of the royal splendor of Solomon is the covenant, no longer placed in the shadow of Israel's unfaithfulness, but in the light of the faithfulness of God that counteracts this unfaithfulness, as he remembers the covenant he made with Israel's forefathers, and now resolves to establish an everlasting covenant in everlasting mercy. It is because of the promise incorporated in this covenant that such joyous utterances are permitted to appear right in the middle of the Old Testament, and that the union of man and woman, taken as an allegory, can be praised accordingly. It is Yahweh's love and faithfulness toward Israel whose praises are being sung here, the incomparable archetype of what can be attained in actual relationships between men and women. The Old Testament speaks truly of the destruction of the sexual relationship, but mindful of its theme of the promise speaks also of its subsequent restoration.

It is of this restoration that the New Testament speaks. Moreover, one passage in particular links the new covenant directly with the union of man and woman, and speaks of these two sets of relationships — between Christ and the church and between man and woman — more impressively and comprehensively than anywhere else. Working outward from here, the whole spectrum of problems is illuminated, and all other relevant New Testament texts may be interpreted accordingly. That passage is Eph 5:21-32.

Be subject to one another out of fear of[3] Christ. (v. 21)

The members of the church are members of Christ's body, and here they are admonished to mutual subjection in the fear of Christ. That is, they should all respect each other in the positions proper to them as members of Christ's body (cf. 1 Corinthians 12), while at the same time acknowledging their collective subjection to the head.

Wives, be subject to your husbands as you are to the Lord. (v. 22)

As Christians are to be subject to each other, and as the church is to be subject to the Lord, so too wives are to be subject to their husbands. It is not, then, the case that the mutual

---

3. NRSV has "reverence." The Greek is literally "fear," reflecting the Hebrew phrase "fear of the Lord," as in Prov 1:7. — Ed.

subjection of Christians amounts to a leveling out. Earthly relationships of submission remain valid for Christians too — indeed, acquire here for the first time their proper meaning. The rider "as you are to the Lord" indicates as much. Christians do not abide by earthly patterns of order because an internal or an external law compels obedience; rather, they display obedience within these patterns of order and, by adhering to them, they thereby obey him who imposes order on everything. Their obedience may be externally indistinguishable from that of non-Christians, but may also suddenly come into conflict with it. With their confession "Jesus Christ is Lord," the first Christians protested against earthly rulers, and suffered persecution and death in consequence. Should any actual form of social order challenge the sovereign claim of Jesus Christ, then Christians must withdraw their obedience to this order. All forms of worldly order can be but pointers toward the divine order, and one must therefore always scrutinize them to discern whether they act legitimately in this respect. What is normative for Christians is not acknowledgment of order as such, or of institutions, but the command of their Lord directed at them within the framework of order; and that means their total submission to the concrete demands made on them by the holy and merciful God in Christ Jesus. However, this command is not imposed on humankind as law, but is experienced as *permission* to obey their Lord, and so to be freed from all law.

If the text now shifts from the central relationship of Jesus Christ and his church to the peripheral relationship of husband and wife, this is not because a new theme is being introduced; rather it is the continuation of the same train of thought. Christians' obedience to their Lord is made manifest in the obedience they practice in the earthly patterns of order within which they are placed and within which they prove their worth as Christians. The text is not interested in the submission of wives or women as such, but only in the witness that such submission can and should give. The apostle addresses women first because it is they,

63

in contrast to men, who in their natural position as wives in relation to husbands reflect the position of Christians, that is, of the church, in relation to their Lord. Thus women are here, so to speak, representative of the reality of that church to which all belong, men and women, that is, husbands and wives, old and young, masters and servants alike. The wife occupies in this respect a privileged position, and what by worldly standards may appear to be a disadvantage becomes in fact a mark of distinction. The husband has first to find his way into the position corresponding to that which the Christian occupies, whereas the wife has the privilege of exemplifying it in what is for her her natural position. What she is being exhorted to do here is actually this.

> For the husband is the head of the wife just as Christ is the head of the church and the Savior [*sōtēr*] of his body.[4] (v. 23)

Even if we do not know "where the notion of the husband being the head of the wife really comes from" (Martin Dibelius, *An die Kolosser, Epheser, an Philemon,* Handbuch zum Neuen Testament 12 [Tübingen: Mohr, 1927], p. 71), here at any rate is the authoritative pronouncement to which we must adhere if we want to know the explanation for this positioning of the husband as head: Christ is head of the church. Whoever is called "head" occupies a position of superiority just as in ordinary parlance the head is the supreme organ governing all others. This notion occurs in the New Testament in both the literal and the figurative sense. Christ is described as the head of the church at two other passages in Ephesians (1:22 and 4:15), and in Colossians (1:18; 2:19), where in addition Christ also appears as the head of his kingdom (the head of all *archē* and all *exousia*, 2:10), as in 1 Cor 11:3 Christ is the head of every man. That the church

---

4. NRSV: "Christ is the head of the church, the body of which he is the Savior." Von Kirschbaum follows a well-attested variant reading in Greek manuscripts. — Ed.

is the body of Christ, and the body is one, is maintained at several other points in Ephesians (2:15; 3:6; 4:4), but without reference to the "head." The notion of Christ as the head and of the church as his body has been attributed to gnostic sources, and numerous similarities with teachings of the mystery religions have also been noted (cf. Heinrich Schlier, *Christus und die Kirche im Epheserbrief* [Tübingen: Mohr, 1930]; and Dibelius, *Epheser,* p. 17).

Yet none of this is particularly helpful in dealing with the question in hand. However close the similarities to non-Christian teachings may be, the fact remains that the writer of this epistle introduced this notion of the "head" in order to describe the wonderful and unique link between Christ and his church. Christ's unity with the church is so completely embracing that the two belong together inseparably like head and body. "She is what she is only as his body, having the very foundation of her being in him as the head, as the inspiration of her growth, and the object to which she attaches herself" (Schlier, *Christus,* p. 53). For it is the wonderful and unique prerogative of the divine "head" not only to rule and govern and lead, but even to create and preserve his body, so that the church does not exist at all except "in him." Here the analogy is pressed beyond its natural limits, as Dibelius observes correctly. The words "and he is the Savior of his body" are not repeated. The man is the head of the woman; within the shared relationship he is the one who leads and decides; it is he who represents the power implicit in proper order: he is not her savior. Rather, woman encounters him as a being of equal rank, both of them formed by God's hand and both of them dependent on God's grace. What counts here is a sense of shared humanity, though also of superiority and submission within the relativity of earthly, creaturely patterns of social order. To what extent, despite this difference and this uniqueness, the relation of man to woman may reflect the relation of Christ to his church is something that this passage will explain further. For the moment, the analogy seems to indicate no more than that both Christ and man represent, in a given pattern of order, the *power* within it.

> Just as the church is subject to Christ, so also wives ought to be, in everything, to their husbands. (v. 24)

Only God the Father and God the Son are the ones in the position of subjecting others. God rendered the creation subject (Rom 8:20), and subjected all things to the Son (1 Cor 15:28). Christians are exhorted to subject themselves one to another (Eph 5:21; cf. 1 Pet 5:5), to the elders and to the authorities (Rom 13:5; Titus 3:1; 1 Pet 2:13); children should be subject to their parents (Eph 6:1-2; Col 3:20; 1 Tim 3:4-5), servants to their masters (Eph 6:5; Col 3:22; Titus 2:9), and wives to their husbands (1 Cor 14:34; Eph 5:22, 24; Col 3:18; 1 Tim 2:11; Titus 2:5; 1 Pet 3:1, 5). Human submission springs from a decision to obey, and hence can become an object of exhortation or admonition. On the one hand, in the case of creation and the angels and powers (1 Pet 3:22), they are subject by nature ("not of its own will," Rom 8:20). On the other hand, Christians, wives, children, and servants make their own decisions, and are by no means the passive objects of the partners they find assigned to them. They are not made subject, they render themselves subject, thereby obeying a divine command. The church is subject to Christ, says our text, thus indicating that its members, in subjecting themselves one to another and to the Lord, only bear witness through their conduct to an existing order of being.

Further, a wife's submission to a husband also encapsulates a statement about being, namely, that God created her a woman and in doing so assigned to her a position of subordination (cf. Gen 2:18-19). Admittedly, the more elevated position of husbands and men and the subjection of wives and women are alleged to be a consequence and sign of sin; however, on the basis of this passage one must contest this allegation. How could a pattern of social order brought about through sin function as

66

an analogy for the pattern of interrelationship between Jesus and his church? Eph 5:22-33 refers explicitly to Gen 2:18-19. Here what is meant is an order established in and with the creation of man and woman, and constitutive of their very being. Yet the Old Testament bears witness to the fact that, with the destruction of the proper form of human relationship through sin, the relation of subjection came to be interpreted differently from its original meaning. The present task is precisely to restore this relation and reclaim its original meaning, which has nothing to do with any notion of the inferiority of women. If a woman were to object to this, maintaining that in her relation to men or to a husband she occupies an inferior position, she would in fact be objecting to her very being as a woman, and hence to her proper destiny as a created being. This is true of each and every woman, just as it is true of each and every man that he is the head of the woman (cf. 1 Cor 11:3).

However, our text does not refer to the man-woman association in general, but to the way in which this general association is to be fulfilled by actual individuals; it speaks of a man and his wife, of the union of two individuals, and thus of marriage. Within marriage a husband and a wife realize the divinely ordained unity of the sexes in the most intimate and complete union possible between human beings. And that is what renders marriage in particular such an apposite analogy. If the general man-woman association finds its proper fulfillment in this particular union, then at the same time the relation of man to woman (and vice versa) is illumined by the fulfillment and the achievement of this union. The promise and command of marriage apply to every man and every woman, for every woman and every man exists to complement the opposite sex. There is truly no neutrality, for even the monk or the nun in their cell cannot escape the fact that their lives are shaped by the notion of a "partner," even though they should never take an actual partner. For they too are created with the hallmark not of independence but of the contrasting dual nature of male and female. How a particular individual chooses to realize this in his or her life will be a matter of individual disposition and of destiny — ultimately indeed of providence — but to escape from this fact is an absolute impossibility. Moreover, it may well be that the single man or woman living alone experiences this encounter more strongly than some men and women do within marriage.

If the text exhorts women to be subject, it does not exhort men, say, to take up their positions as heads, but to . . . love their wives.

> Husbands, love your wives, just as Christ loved . . . (v. 25a)

Now, paradoxically, the husband becomes an analogue precisely at the point where the analogy breaks down. For what constitutes the love of Christ is revealed in the following words:

> and gave himself up for her [the church], in order to make her holy by cleansing her with the washing of water by the word, so as to present the church to himself in splendor, without spot or wrinkle or anything of the kind — yes, so that she might be holy and without blemish. (vv. 25b-27)

This love is wonderful and unique. It is the divine love of him who is the "savior" of his church. He has so "chosen" his church, and made her his own, that he called her into life through his death. He has sanctified her and liberated her from darkness into the glory of his light. He has clothed her with his splendor. Now she has been purified, and in this "alien righteousness," imputed to her through the word and baptism, without spot or wrinkle, she is in truth holy and without blemish. That is Christ's loving election of his church as his "companion." The tie that binds Christ and his church is indestructible, eternal, because it is guaranteed by eternal love.

How can the love of man become an analogy of this love? There can be no question of repetition or imitation. The text of

Ephesians now takes a turn that, left on our own, we should certainly not have anticipated. It tells us that it is the natural love of the husband for his wife that is the creaturely reflection of this divine love.

> In the same way, husbands should love their wives as they do their own bodies. He who loves his wife loves himself. (v. 28)

Thus no sacrifice is being demanded here, such as a readiness to lay down one's life, or even to renounce natural stirrings of emotion — on the contrary, it is precisely the natural love of a husband for his wife that becomes the object of exhortation. In loving his wife, the husband loves himself, or in other words, in this love and its fulfillment in marriage the husband emerges in all the fullness of his nature as a man in ways hardly to be found in any other sphere of his existence. The text, far from placing this love under any "suspicion," takes it seriously — so seriously, indeed, as to discern the very image or reflection of the love of Christ in it. It specifies simply the one requirement, that this love should be as complete as if the husband were treasuring his own body, and hence affirming his "other half" as unreservedly as if she were an actual part of himself. This is the true meaning of love — to allow the other person's existence to become a condition of one's own existence. The husband has not bestowed on his wife the gift of life itself, he has not "redeemed" her, and he is also unable to transform her as Christ's love does the church. Were the husband to think himself capable of this he would undoubtedly be disappointed; he would mold his partner according to his own image, he would "perhaps" invent her and then one day surely wake up disappointed. No, what counts is a true meeting of person with person, of husband with wife, and what is absolutely decisive is whether one truly knows the other person and loves the other in his or her singular individuality — whether the "I" truly finds its "Thou."

Opinions will differ as to whether such a genuine encounter

is a matter of chance, whether it falls within the range of personal decision making, or whether it is a matter of a divine calling. However, what is indicated to us here is that if this encounter is to form the basis of a genuine and proper union of two people, if it is *the* encounter between this man and this woman, then it must fulfill the condition of the man loving the woman as himself. Holy Scripture clearly thinks far more responsibly and seriously about this matter than Christian theology or the church have been accustomed to doing. Here the natural love of a husband for his wife becomes the object of apostolic exhortation; here this pivotal realm of sexual love, instead of being denigrated as belonging to "Eros," is picked out as worthy of bearing apt witness. Hence the union of two individuals is not perceived from the outset merely as the "yoke" that is to be borne in patience and in hope; rather, Holy Scripture itself recognizes in it a fulfillment. "But from the beginning it was not so," says Jesus to his disciples (Matt 19:8), not meaning thereby that there was once a time when divorce or marital breakdown did not exist, but referring rather to that union of husband and wife that is in its essence indestructible, and quoting in that regard Gen 2:24 (Matt 19:3-4).

Our text tells us which particular fulfillment is ultimately being implied here, namely, the union of Christ with his church. In the light of this latter relationship, however, the relationship of husband and wife is no longer construed in Old Testament terms, but is perceived in its primeval beauty. Now certainly this implies that each and every fulfillment granted to us here on earth is necessarily besmirched by the stain of sin and therefore also of suffering. Yet this most emphatically does not mean that one should give in forthwith and ignore the weight of seriousness and degree of urgency with which this text in Ephesians summons husband and wife to unconditional union and total affirmation. Ephesians 5 is as much part of the Bible as Gen 2:18-19 or the Song of Songs. As Franz-J. Leenhardt observes correctly (*La Place de la Femme dans l'Eglise d'après le Nouveau Testament*

[1948], p. 26; recently published in a German translation, *Die Stellung der Frau im Neuen Testament,* Kirchliche Zeitfragen 24 [Zurich: Zwingli, 1949]):

> This point is vital for understanding the full significance of Christian marriage, which is really founded in Christ, because Christ's love is the basic principle underlying the love of husband and wife. A man and a woman can only truly love each other if they know that their love has something in it of the great love with which they are loved. It is then that human love truly attains its full measure in breadth, in intensity, in depth, and in duration. Paul tried to make this clear. He also included in his exhortation to married couples this comparison of their union with the union of Christ and the church, of which they should become by faith "the imitators," that is, the beneficiaries.

What emerges clearly from what follows is that Leenhardt wants to apply the notion of *imitatio,* imitation, to husband and wife in a manner that overlooks the false parallels produced by the analogy between the two relationships. Otherwise he would be unable to say (p. 28):

> The Christian man, knowing what is Christ's relationship with the church, will take this as the pattern for his devotion toward his wife. And the Christian woman, in turn, knowing the relationship of the church to Christ, will take this as the pattern for her affection for husband and conformity to him. As Christ lives for the church, and the church for Christ, so he lives for her and she lives through him.

"So he lives for her and she lives through him" — is it at all possible to say this of the union of any two human beings? Surely this would be to blur the fundamental difference between the love of Christ and the love of man? Surely our text is much

71

more circumspect here, consciously describing the love of a husband as an earthly, natural love: he is to love his wife as his own body (but it is not asserted that she *is* his body), as himself. To be sure, we discern in this the commandment to love one's neighbor as oneself, but with specific reference to the fact of *this* neighbor — the wife — being destined for this husband. Any overly hasty generalization at this point would obliterate what is very particular in the apostle's exhortation.

And sadly, all too often this has happened. Perhaps the church would not be facing today's countless broken marriages in quite such a bewildered and helpless way if it had been able to listen more closely at this point, and been able to read the relevant texts in a less prejudiced way. For then it would urgently exhort both partners, prior to entering on the marriage bond, to examine whether the man really recognizes the woman, and the woman the man, as the one whose existence belongs to them as if it were their very own; whether the "I" has truly discovered its "Thou," and whether here, in all the defects of this sinful world, there is nevertheless some trace of Adam's exultation when God gave him woman. Admittedly, even when this question is answered in all good faith positively, there remains the possibility of human error and delusion. Nevertheless, that in no way absolves us from harkening to the commandment that stems from Ephesians 5 and from being held answerable by it. All the other considerations relevant to a decision to enter into marriage become a legitimate focus of concern only when this fundamental question has been asked and answered. There may be reasons in support of embarking on a marriage even when it is undeniable that this love is not there after all. Yet even a marriage undertaken in those circumstances must be held accountable under the apostle's teaching. From the outset it is a vulnerable marriage. Where the husband loves his wife as his own body, then all her wants and desires become his too. That love by its nature constitutes faithfulness. And by its nature it is exclusive. Hence, in truth, monogamy can be protected and nurtured only where this kind of love is alive and flourishing. The requirement of monogamy finds its only justification in the fact that an indissoluble bond unites Christ with his church in one body. And it is precisely because of this that marriage rooted in love becomes an appropriate model for the "great secret."

Any distancing of the one from the other — or any hostile distancing, at least — is then an impossibility.

> For no one ever hates his own body, but he nourishes and tenderly cares for it, just as Christ does for the church. (v. 29)

This verse points forward unmistakably to v. 31, to the quotation from the creation narrative (Gen 2:24). In that union of husband and wife that is rooted in genuine and therefore lasting love, something of a vocation in accord with creation itself blazes out. "This at last is bone of my bones and flesh of my flesh" (Gen 2:23). Such is the affinity between his wife and him that the husband recognizes in her his own flesh, a person like himself and yet not simply a reproduction of himself but the "Thou" to whom his "I" responds. Of course, "all flesh is as grass," and the tie that binds two people together culminates in death. There is no everlasting love and faithfulness here, only earthly love and faithfulness, which are nevertheless capable of becoming an image of the everlasting tie, namely, the love and faithfulness of Christ, which never ceases.

> Because we are members of his body, of his flesh and of his bones.[5] (v. 30)

---

5. Von Kirschbaum adds the gloss: "of his flesh and of his bones," not in the NRSV or Nestle-Aland's *Novum Testamentum Graece* (26th ed.), but in some Western Fathers and "Western" manuscripts of the Greek New Testament, and noted in NRSV margin. See the corrected 3rd ed. of the United Bible Society's *Greek New Testament* (1983). — Ed.

This pronouncement is one of joy, and at the same time the text switches suddenly to use the term "we." We, that is, we Christians, may say that. It is the miracle of the incarnation of Christ who through his resurrection has transposed our flesh into the kingdom of the Father, so that we can validly assert: "our citizenship is in heaven" (Phil 3:20). That is how closely he has bound himself to us, and binds himself to us every day anew in the Holy Spirit. Thus he becomes one with us.

> For this reason a man will leave his father and mother and be joined to his wife, and the two will become one flesh. (v. 31)

The Old Testament, quoted here, presumably has in mind, in the first instance, the husband leaving his parental home after meeting his future wife, and now renouncing all previous ties for her sake in order to form with her the tie that will unite the two of them, and that has been precipitated by the inexorable necessities of true love. Yet if this were all that was intended, one would be forced to ask, in some astonishment, why this procedure should be accorded such significance — and our text furnishes us with the answer.

> This is a great mystery, and I am applying it to Christ and the church. (v. 32)

The leaving of home and family that is only hinted at and faintly anticipated in the creation story is that of the man who leaves his father's house for our sakes and who, "though he was in the form of God, did not regard equality with God as something to be exploited, but emptied himself, taking the form of a slave, being born in human likeness. And being found in human form . . ." (Phil 2:5-7). That is the great and crucial secret: the Word became flesh. Now our flesh is no longer lost, now it is sanctified. The world remains ignorant of this fact, but his church does not, for he himself tells it. Those who hear his word and

74

JESUS CHRIST AND THE CHURCH

accept it in faith are permitted too to recognize the earthly secrets in which the greatest of secrets is reflected. One such earthly secret is the creation of humanity in the form of male and female, their divinely ordained unity, and its fulfillment in marriage. It is a reality that becomes apparent only in the light of that quite different reality.

> Each of you, however, should love his wife as himself, and a wife should respect her husband. (v. 33)

In the light of the covenant of grace, the husband may love his wife as himself — indeed, he is placed under an obligation to live his humanity in the relationship, and to make the union of husband and wife a reality. Sexual love is here called to account as to whether it is "legitimate" love, namely, this unconditional and total affirmation of the "Thou." Only when the wife is truly "companion" to her husband, and thus truly remedies his loneliness, does she regain her original place of honor as a "helper." Yet in a genuine encounter the wife's response can only be one of acknowledgment and affirmation of her "companion" in turn. On the one hand, our text grants the initiative to the husband, thereby indicating something of the iconlike character of his position. On the other hand, her role, permeated by the responsibility for their union that she too shares, and to exactly the same degree, with the husband, is to be truly his wife in a correspondingly unconditional way, and thus to accord to him the position that is his by right. To "respect" or "fear" him, as a response to his love, can only mean to take him seriously in his love for her, and hence to acknowledge him as her husband and her "head."

And in the case of his wife too there can be seen once again at this point the analogous significance of her natural role: the church responds to the love of Christ with the Yes of faith and gratitude, and acknowledges him as her head. That he is precisely that, that is the good news, that is the light that shines in the

75

darkness. It shines too into the gloomy and basically flawed realm of the husband-wife relationship, and this, illumined by the light, is once again able to recover features of its original, divinely ordained purpose. Where this is recognized, where the Word of God is once again heard in this respect too, then clarity will replace current confusion, the sexual life will be viewed — and then lived — with a new sense of responsibility. Yet because this realm of love between husband and wife is at the heart of the relation between man and woman in general, to clarify it will also contribute to an understanding of the general relation of the sexes and, in particular, of the position of women.

# ❖ 2 ❖

# WOMEN IN THE LIFE OF THE CHURCH UNDER THE NEW COVENANT

IN addition to the twelve apostles, "women" are mentioned (Luke 8:2-3) as belonging to Jesus' circle during his ministry here on earth — women who are close to him in suffering (Mark 15:40 and parallels), death, and resurrection (Mark 16:1-2 and parallels; John 20:1, 11-12). Summoned by Jesus by means of a miraculous healing or an exorcism, they follow him from Galilee to Jerusalem and Golgotha, stand watch beneath the cross, are present at his burial, and on Easter morning they see the empty tomb. It is to these women, or to some of them (according to John, only to Mary Magdalene), that the risen Christ first appears. In addition, they are described as serving Jesus' needs and supporting him from their property. Some of them we get to know by name: Salome; Joanna, wife of Chuza, Herod's attendant; Susanna; and a series of Marys, among whom, in addition to Mary the mother of Jesus, particular mention is made of Mary of Magdala or Mary Magdalene, from whom Jesus had driven seven demons (Luke 8:2).

On the one hand, these women are clearly distinguished from the twelve disciples: the Lord does not take them to one side, as he so often does with his disciples, in order to impart teaching and induct them into the mystery of the way he is called to follow; he does not grant them the power *(exousia)* to perform miracles, as he does to his disciples; and he does not send them, as he sends his disciples, "to the lost sheep of Israel" (Matt 10:6). On the other hand, the women stand out clearly from the "masses" or "multitudes of people" (Mark 8:2; 10:1; etc.) that regularly gather around Jesus, see him and at the same time fail to perceive, hear him and at the same time fail to understand him, and then once again disperse. This demarcation from the Twelve on the one hand and the nameless crowds on the other hand locates these women unmistakably in the same position as the church, that is, between the apostles and the world. Of course, the Twelve also belong to his church, and the multitudes surrounding him have been summoned by him and must therefore not be excluded. Nevertheless, the women come across in the Gospels as representative of the church drawn out by the Lord from among Israel.

We hear nothing about a direct relationship between the women and the Twelve. Jesus is the center and unifying focus of his followers. Only on the cross does the dying Lord point Mary toward the apostle and the apostle to Mary (John 19:26-27). That the circle of the "Twelve" consisted only of men, with Jesus summoning women to join it, can hardly be explained on the grounds of the Lord not wishing to depart from convention, and of a wandering lifestyle being too arduous for women, as claimed by Ds. Rasker ("De Vrouw, Haar Plaats en Roeping," in *Onze Tijd* [Callenbach], p. 17). For the women (including, moreover, married women!) *do* belong to Jesus' circle, and do accompany him on his arduous journeys. That the circle of apostles consists exclusively of men should be understood rather as deriving from the special task that the Lord lays on the Twelve and for which he himself equips them with special authority. The risen Lord will dispatch them as his ambassadors to "all nations"; in other words, he will bestow on them an "office" that is to be temporally and spatially limited only by the End and the ends of the earth (see Markus Barth, *Der Augenzeuge* [The Witness] [Zollikon-Zurich: Evangelischer Verlag, 1946], p. 254). In doing so, however, the Lord clearly differentiates these representatives of the congregation of Israel from the rest of the community, appointing them as his representatives, and thereby makes these particular members of the church quite distinct from the rest of the community. The apostles are to be *leaders* of the church; they are to represent the "head" of the church to the church, a church made up, moreover, of both Jews and Gentiles. This "apostolic office," with its special authority, is granted only to men. The spiritual order is here a reflection of the natural order: the husband is head of the wife, the man of the woman. The woman, however, occupies the position of the *church,* subjecting herself to this head.

The women too receive a commission from the Lord. On Easter morning the risen Lord encounters the women first (Matt 28:9), and they kneel before him and touch his feet, thereby announcing their readiness to be his maidservants and to enter his service. The Lord accepts them into his service and sends them to the "brethren" with a particular charge. According to John (John 20:14ff.) it is Mary Magdalene, returning distraught from the empty tomb, who sees the risen Lord and recognizes him when he calls her by name. However, he forbids her to touch his body on the ground that he is not yet ascended to the Father. Instead she is charged with going to the "brethren" and telling them that he is to ascend. Mary goes and announces to the brethren, " 'I have seen the Lord,' and she told them that he had said these things to her." The very first announcement of the resurrection comes therefore from the mouth of a woman. According to Mark 16:11, "they [the disciples] would not believe"; according to Luke 24:11, "these words seemed to them an idle tale, and they did not believe them." (Moreover, according to these two evangelists, it is only the angels who bear witness to the women of the fact of the resurrection, and it is they who send them.)

Further light is thrown on the difference between the apostles and the rest of the church by the fact that whereas Mary is forbidden to touch the risen Lord, his disciples not only may but

79

must do so (Luke 24:39; John 20:20, 27). They, whom he is to send out to all nations, are his witnesses who can show proof of their authority through being able to testify: "what was from the beginning, what we have heard, what we have seen with our eyes, what we have looked at and touched with our hands" (1 John 1:1). Mary, however, as representative of the congregation of Israel, must not insist on the fact of Jesus' belonging physically to Israel. During his life on earth, men and women of Israel were permitted to touch the incarnate Lord. The Old Testament knows of no touching of the "holy" by women. They were excluded from ritual service of the holy. Yet when the holy is in their midst, the proscription lapses. Women — Mary, Elizabeth, Hannah — are the first to experience it, and to touch it, as when the menstruating woman touches Jesus, or women anoint his body with oil. Israel according to the flesh must be reborn through the Spirit. Hence Mary's way now leads her to the "brethren." On them the risen Lord breathes the Holy Spirit and installs them in their priestly office, for the forgiveness and retention of sins (John 20:22). Only when the chosen among the Gentiles are brought into Israel and the apostles have completed their task will Israel too, the new Israel, hasten as a "bride" toward her bridegroom. This promise belongs with the prohibition on touching the risen Lord.

Mary receives, then, from the risen Lord a temporally and spatially limited task. We are now in a position to reject the claim, advanced by Hippolytus, that she was appointed "apostle of the apostles." Equally, though, we may now affirm that Israel's right of the firstborn is confirmed by the risen Lord in his appearing first to Mary and only subsequently to the disciples.

In John's Gospel "Mary" undoubtedly features as someone accorded a particular preference. She clearly reflects the features of the church drawn by the Lord from among Israel, and consequently there are frequent occasions on which he contrasts her with the disciples in such a way as to hold her up as an example to them. A particularly clear example of this is the story of the anointing of Jesus in Bethany (John 12:1-8). It is Mary the sister

80

of Lazarus and Martha who anoints Jesus' feet with a pound of expensive ointment and dries his feet with her hair. Judas Iscariot complains about this (according to Matthew 26 and Mark 14 it is the disciples as a whole who complain): the money would have been better spent on the poor. But Jesus defends Mary: "Leave her alone. She bought it so that she might keep it for the day of my burial. You always have the poor with you, but you do not always have me" (vv. 7-8). With her prophetic action in anointing him Mary glorifies the dying king of Israel. With her extravagant devotion she bears witness to her love and gratitude, thus forming a pure contrast to the impure Judas, who is a "thief." He is unwilling to give the Lord everything, while at the same time stealing from him the honor that is his proper due. Judas's way leads inexorably to the execution of the Lord. The only future in the community, in the church, lies with this Mary, with the apostolic office exercised in accordance with her wholehearted devotion. Thus Mary's action acquires normative significance for the disciples.

Meanwhile, as is well known, Jesus also, according to Mark and Luke, once held up a woman as an example to his disciples: the "poor widow" who put everything she had into the treasury (Mark 12:41-44; Luke 21:1-4). And when Luke tells the story of the two sisters, Mary and Martha, at Bethany, there too Mary's conduct is portrayed as having been held up by the Lord himself as exemplary, as the one thing that was needful (Luke 10:33-42; see also the parables of Jesus, 15:8-9; 18:2-3). Martha serves Jesus when he comes to her house as a guest, and asks him to tell Mary to help her. But Jesus refuses. He acknowledges the pains that Martha is taking, yet at the same time tells her that Mary, who has sat down at his feet to listen to him speaking, is doing the one thing necessary. "Mary has chosen the better part, which will not be taken away from her." Martha's service is not rejected, yet it gains its value from Mary's listening to the word of the Lord. Both sisters represent the church, and both serve the Lord (it would be a mistake to try to play off the contemplative against the activist at

81

this point!), but it is Mary who does what absolutely must be done when the Lord speaks: she *listens*. If Martha were to want to query that, she would be overlooking the Lord present in his word. The one thing necessary would then not occur.

Lazarus's two sisters appear in John's Gospel also (John 11), and here too it is Mary who is, so to speak, central to the action. They summon the Lord to help their sick brother, Jesus responds, and when he appears, Lazarus has already been dead for four days. Martha hurries forward to meet him, lamenting, and Jesus tells her that her brother will rise again. Martha takes this to mean in the general resurrection on the Day of Judgment. Jesus, however, points to himself: "I am the resurrection and the life" (v. 25). And Martha acknowledges — with the very words used by Peter in Matthew 16! — that Jesus is "the Messiah, the Son of God, the one coming into the world." She calls her sister Mary; Mary comes, falls down weeping at Jesus' feet, and, like her sister Martha, says: "Lord, if you had been here, my brother would not have died" (John 11:32). And when Jesus sees Mary weeping, and also the Jews who came with her, then he groans in his spirit and is troubled. What moves him is not the grief of bereavement experienced by Mary and the Jews, but that they both, Mary and the Jews, succumb through their grief to the power of death while he, the lord of life and death, stands there before them. The miracle happens — Lazarus rises from the dead. "Many of the Jews, therefore, who had come with Mary and had seen what Jesus did, believed in him" (v. 45). Clearly, here again the church drawn from Israel is reflected in the figure of Mary, and it is she who portrays the polarity between Jesus and his church. The way in which the figure of a woman lends itself for use as an apt analogy emerges most clearly in a situation of direct encounter with Jesus.

John tells us of one other encounter between Jesus and a woman. She remains anonymous, being called simply after the people to whom she belongs, the country that she lives in: it is a woman from Samaria, the Samaritan woman (John 4:1-42). The encounter takes place on Israel's boundary with the Gentiles.

82

Samaria had belonged previously to the northern kingdom in Israel, but had now become a gentile province. Among the gentile colonists there still lived remnants of the old Israelite population, although they no longer used the temple in Jerusalem, having instead their own temple on Mount Gerizim. For this reason the Jews despised the Samaritans and had nothing to do with them.

The first person whom Jesus meets in this area is this woman, drawing water from Jacob's well. Jesus speaks to her and asks for a drink of water. He breaks through the barrier erected between Jews and Samaritans, and he breaks through the barrier that, according to the custom of the time, existed between men and women. The woman is astonished. He reveals himself to her as the source of waters that never run dry, and when she thirsts after this, he tells her to fetch her husband and then return with him. Here, though, Jesus uncovers the corruption in the life of this woman; she had had five husbands, and the man she was now living with was not her husband.

This woman's lot mirrors the fate of Samaria. Again and again this people had broken its covenant with Yahweh, gone lusting after false gods (1 Kgs 13:32; Ezek 23:45), and was now living, without any authorization to do so, separate from the Jews, from whom salvation was to come. And now what Ezekiel had prophesied was happening, was coming true: "I will restore their fortunes. . . . Samaria and her daughters shall return to their former state" (16:53-55). God remembers his covenant. That is why Jesus says, "The hour is coming, and is now here, when the true worshipers will worship the Father in spirit and truth" (John 4:23). The question of the temple becomes redundant. Now the prophecy is fulfilled, now salvation is here. And Jesus reveals himself as Israel's Messiah.

The woman hurries into the town and tells people what had happened to her: "He told me everything I have ever done" (v. 39). And many believe in him because of the woman's testimony. They go out to meet Jesus and ask him to stay with them. He stays for two days and then has to return to Judea. "And many more believed because of his word. They said to the woman: 'It is no longer because of what you said that we believe, for we have heard for ourselves, and we know that this is truly the Savior [*sōtēr*] of the world.'" This does nothing to diminish the value of the woman's own testimony. It was she who brought the news of Jesus to Samaria, it was to her that the Lord first spoke, it was to her that he revealed himself as Messiah. She remains with her message within the framework of Israelite understanding, and only their first direct encounter with the Lord reveals to the Samaritans that he is the Christ, the savior of the world. The woman is not guilty of any error in her story, but her words are outclassed. Their true meaning becomes apparent only in the words of Jesus himself.

It is undeniable that Jesus' first contact with the church that he seeks to gather out of Samaria is with the Samaritan woman. She is no "Mary" — the encounter is altogether more distanced in character, and there is hardly any trace of the sense of intimacy that one finds between Israel and the Lord. This woman does not fall at Jesus' feet, she does not touch him. Yet she is addressed by him and feels herself to be known by him. In her sinful life she is confronted by the word of the Lord. When Jesus enters into her life, all her sinful past is done away with, for the savior has appeared. The hour has come, as it has for this woman, so too for Samaria: with the coming of Jesus, the light dawns for this people too (cf. Acts 8:14).

Finally, the encounter reported in the Gospels (Mark 7:24-30; Matt 15:21-28) between Jesus and the Greek/Syrophoenician woman, a Gentile, belongs to the present context. She runs after Jesus — he has not called her or spoken to her — and cries out for help for her daughter who is tormented by a demon. Jesus does not respond. She continues to cry out, and the disciples beg him to "drive her off" (Matt 15:23; in the Greek text this is the same word as to "redeem" or "deliver" her). Jesus replies, however, that he is come only to the lost sheep of the house of Israel. The woman comes up to him, prostrates herself before him, and pleads: "Lord, help me." He, however, says to her that she wants to take some-

84

thing that does not belong to her, it belongs to the "children." She accepts this, acknowledges Israel's prior claim, and asks merely for the crumbs that fall from their master's table. At this Jesus replies: "Woman, great is your faith! Let it be done for you as you wish." And in the same hour her daughter was cured.

Once again it is a woman in whom people's response to the coming of Jesus is reflected. According to Jesus' own words this gentile woman has great faith: she accepts that she does not belong to the "children of the house"; yet despite her rejection by Jesus she clings to her hope that his power is strong enough to reach beyond its original sphere of operation and to embrace her too. This faithful hope satisfies Jesus, and he heals her daughter — from a distance (as with the Roman centurion's servant). This woman too, in bringing all her personal need to Jesus, and experiencing for herself the personal help he can give, represents at the same time the first outstretching toward him of the gentile world, the first germ of his church drawn from among all nations. The hour has not yet come; the focus of his attention must for the present remain Israel alone. Yet the light that shines with his coming already illuminates the darkness. Already there appears, in response to this mother's cry for help, a miraculous sign of his merciful love.

Thus all these incidents in which Jesus encounters women, as well as being personal encounters and ones that incorporate particular cases of practical help and support, are also symbolic representations of Jesus' encounter with his church, drawn first from among Israel, but then from Samaria and the gentile world also. Moreover, it is significant for any proper understanding of the man-woman relationship in general that during the time of Jesus' sojourn on earth, and while he was summoning women to join his followers, was healing them, forgiving their sins, and revealing himself to them as Israel's Messiah, that for these women the question of their relationship to men, and also to their husbands, appeared to fade in importance. In Jesus they had before them *the* man, summoning his church to him as his partner. Those who were called, both men and women, found in him the Lord of their lives, and submission to this Lord causes all other forms of submission to fade into the background. What dominated the foreground was the matter in hand, and here we find the apostle's claim already anticipated: "There is no longer male and female; for all of you are one in Christ Jesus" (Gal 3:28). The limits and at the same time the fulfillment of all earthly frameworks of order become visible. This has nothing to do with a movement for the emancipation of women because what they are doing is responding to the summons of Jesus. And that is exactly the reason why this novel movement toward him is the most revolutionary ever in women's history. Women's subordinate position in relation to men is not abolished — rather, women can see that it is precisely through their obedience to the Lord (and to his representative, the apostle Paul) that their natural existence as women is privileged to function as an analogy for their existence as Christians in the church of Jesus Christ.

It is precisely this that is important: that the natural order or relationship between men and women is not abolished through the coming of Jesus into the world, but that on the contrary it is now revealed for the first time in its true meaning and hence in its true dignity. The Lord does not take his followers out of the world; on the contrary, he sends them into the world so that they can bear witness to him. They are to be the "light of the world" that he has lit, and proclaim his lordship. Illuminated by this message, all forms of earthly order may now stand in his service. Jesus does not abolish the Mosaic law, and he does not water down God's commandments — rather, he uncovers their true meaning and shows people up for the failures they are. Thus the relationship between men and women is drawn into the relentless light of the "But I say to you . . ." pronouncements. "You have heard that it was said, 'You shall not commit adultery.' But I say to you that everyone who looks at a woman with lust has already committed adultery with her in his heart" (Matt 5:27-28). And when the Pharisees ask him (Matt 19:3) whether it is lawful for a man to divorce his wife for any cause,

86

Jesus counters with the question: "Have you not read that the one who made them at the beginning [*ap' archēs*] 'made them male and female,' and said, 'For this reason a man shall leave his father and mother and be joined to his wife, and the two shall become one flesh'? So they are no longer two, but one flesh. Therefore what God has joined together, let no one separate" (vv. 4-6).

Jesus shows the Pharisees here the "original" order as created and ordained by God "in the beginning" (Gen 2:18-19), namely, an order of interdependence between man and woman. The bond prophesied there is in its essence an indestructible and therefore indissoluble bond. Man and woman, as joined together by God, are one. Human sin has destroyed this unity. But the one who now speaks to the Pharisees and interprets the Mosaic law to them ("But I say to you . . .") has restored the damaged order; he has fulfilled God's intention. The tie that binds Jesus Christ and his church is an indestructible and indissoluble tie because it is sustained by the love of Christ. In this bond, though, we can discern the human bond between man and woman in its original meaning, with the husband loving his wife and the wife responding to this love, and with the partnership between this man and this woman forming an analogy for the partnership between Jesus Christ and his church. Where this holds good, "adultery" and "divorce" are impossible. If they do emerge as possibilities, what this means is that the original unity has been lost, that in respect of God's commandment we humans are failures. This is what Jesus lays bare. He poses the question of marriage so starkly that there is nothing equivocal about it any more, and his disciples(!) can only say: If that is how things are, then it is better not to be married. Humankind would be simply abandoned to its fate, were it not for the fact that the person speaking here, the "But I . . . ," is the Lord going on his way to lay down his life for humanity and thereby to save it. He, the savior of his body, becomes one with humankind. It is into *this* union that he seeks to call people by revealing to them the fragility of the unions they themselves enter into. Taken up by him into this union, their relationship can then once again function properly as an analogy. It is the "new life" in the forgiveness of sin that Jesus is indicating to them here, precisely by upholding God's commandment so inflexibly.

The Pharisees do not understand him. In the temple (John 8:3-4), they bring him a woman taken in adultery, and ask him what they should do with her. According to the law of Moses she should be stoned. Thus either this penalty must be carried out, or the law of Moses must be flouted: those are the only alternatives. The Pharisees intend, of course, to "tempt" Jesus with this dilemma. But Jesus counters by asking them what right they have to pronounce judgment on this sinner. "Let anyone among you who is without sin be the first to throw a stone at her" (v. 7). And one after another they went away. He, however, the only one who is without sin, and who thus in truth is *the* judge, does not condemn the woman — he dismisses her: "Go your way, and from now on do not sin again." Did Jesus, then, weaken the force of God's commandment, and exculpate this woman? He met God's demands fully, and he also fulfilled them on behalf of this woman, which is why he could forgive her, and acquit her, for it was in that way that he could claim her for *his* commandment. The stones that were to have struck this woman would strike him. At the end of the chapter we read: "So they picked up stones to throw at him, but Jesus hid himself and went out of the temple" (v. 59). His hour had not yet come.

Because of this mission fulfilled by the obedience of Jesus Christ, husband and wife may *live*. In their gratitude for the salvation that has befallen them their life together will testify to it, and husband and wife together will attest the grace bestowed on them.

It is emphatically the wife who is addressed in this connection in the New Testament. First Peter speaks of a mode of existence of the wife that, while not being a witness exactly, is nevertheless a "sign" that can "win" for the Word. We read that

88

wives should be subject to their husbands "so that, even if some of them do not obey the word, they may be won over without a word by their wives' conduct, when they see the purity and reverence of your lives" (1 Pet 3:1-2). Submission is fulfilled here in "purity and reverence." Such women, the epistle continues, will not adorn themselves with outward adorning, but their adorning will be "the inner self with the lasting beauty of a gentle and quiet spirit" (v. 4). They are not graced, then, with a specifically feminine virtue, but with *the* Christian "virtue": the new person born again in Christ! That is how the holy women were "adorned" who hoped in God and rendered themselves subject to their husbands, and also Sarah, who obeyed Abraham, calling him Lord. It is not Abraham's son who is presented in this text as the subject of the right conduct that casts out fear, but "Sarah's daughter." Although Christ's law applies to all, men and women, husbands and wives, nevertheless it seems to be the wife who is primarily addressed here. It is only the woman who is able in her natural position as wife to reflect the position of the Christian. By acknowledging her position in respect of her husband — not as a law that is burdensome but as a place assigned to her in particular by God himself, a place that she affirms because of its special distinction as a lived parable, and within the restrictions placed on her — she will be free from the angst associated with the weaker party. For she now exists in the security and peace of a grateful creature, obeying the law of Christ and thus the law of grace.

This dependence of the wife on grace in her natural existence is, from a Christian point of view, her "advantage." If she knows this, and if she herself lives nourished by grace, then her way of expressing this as a wife is to render herself subject, thereby becoming herself a "sign." The husband too, incidentally, as a member of the church cannot aspire to be more than a "weaker vessel" (1 Pet 3:7, NRSV margin), for in the church there are only "weaker vessels." Hence, because the wife is the symbolic representative of the church, he must honor her also as one of the "heirs of the gracious gift of life," and his prayers would be hindered, would be an "offense," if he were to fail to honor his wife.

Thus the church sanctifies otherwise profane or human roles, and life in its outward aspects stands under the law of Christ that controls the church. Thus the external aspects can also be seen and understood in their meaningful connection to the central event. All spheres of human life are included here, and no area is beyond reach of this sanctification. For it is the whole person, the person as soul *and* body, who is addressed by the Word of God. For the relationship between the sexes, however, this means that there is no encounter between husband and wife that does not come under the divine command, and that therefore even the physical union of husband and wife stands beneath it. "And the two become one flesh" stands as promise and demand over sexual life too. Paul says as much with incomparable clarity in 1 Corinthians (ch. 6). The Corinthians appear to be of the mistaken opinion that they can treat sexual intercourse purely as a matter of sensual gratification, comparable in that respect to eating and drinking. And now they are told that a person's body belongs to the Lord. "Do you not know that your bodies are members of Christ?" (v. 15). The whole person is the property of the Lord, body and soul together. If they know that, how then can they commit fornication? "Do you not know that whoever is united to a prostitute becomes one body with her? For it is said, 'The two shall be one flesh'" (v. 16). There is no sexual act without obligation. When a man and a woman unite physically, they are subject to the demands of the law of marriage; they are judged according to the measure of unreserved and total mutual affirmation, of that union that is by its very nature indestructible. Only where the I seeks and finds its Thou, the human being its fellow human being, the husband his wife, only, in other words, where physical union is an expression of genuine love, do we have a human encounter and one that can be distinguished in its own right from a merely animal act. If one's partner merely provides one with sensual gratification, then

90

he or she is degraded, the human being's very humanity is destroyed, the intimacy between husband and wife is robbed of its credibility, and what should constitute its promise becomes a judgment on it. "Do you not know that your body is a temple of the Holy Spirit?" "You were bought with a price" by Christ. Therefore it is incompatible with one's nature as a Christian to throw away one's body. It is precisely through one's body that one should and may glorify him who saved us. It is precisely in one's sexuality that one experiences the demand to treasure the secret of creation. The only thing that one can really allow to count here is the command: "Shun fornication."

Paul's worry that members of the Corinthian church would like to succumb to the fornication customary among the Gentiles while at the same time "spiritualizing" their marriages causes him to write: "Because of cases of sexual immorality, each man should have his own wife and each woman her own husband" (7:2). Marriage means a shared spiritual *and* physical life. To seek to change its meaning to a purely spiritual sharing between husband and wife would be to destroy the unity of husband and wife. It is the whole human being who is here seeking out his or her whole fellow human being. An only partial affirmation runs the risk of infidelity. And it would for this reason constitute a misunderstanding both of what the bond between two people should be and what the physical union of husband and wife means. It is precisely here that the mutual interdependence of husband and wife finds its most intimate expression. It is not the wife who controls her body but the husband. Equally it is not the husband who controls his body but the wife. Where we have a genuine case of two people sharing their lives in all intimacy, the wants and desires of the I will be the wants and desires of the Thou, and vice versa. That Paul speaks in this connection of "fasting" and "praying" indicates how threatened this area of life is, and how it can be lived responsibly only in a state of the highest awareness.

"If her husband dies, she [the wife] is discharged from the law concerning the husband" (Rom 7:2). Thus death already limits the intimate sharing possible between two people. There is no everlasting love and everlasting faithfulness on earth. The word of the Lord, "For in the resurrection they neither marry nor are given in marriage, but are like angels in heaven" (Matt 22:30), shows that this pattern of relationship between men and women belongs to the transitoriness of the world and will pass away along with it, and indeed the process has already begun. The end is near. And the old order has passed away. In the life and death of Jesus Christ the fullness of time was completed. Christians are in a position to know that and to bear witness to it to the rest of the world. They know of the limitations inherent in all earthly existence and of how they are transcended in the everlasting and immortal life. Hence it may occur that individual members of the church decide to remain celibate because they are "anxious about the affairs of the Lord, how to please the Lord" and not for the "affairs of the world, how to please his wife [or husband]" (1 Cor 7:32-33). To remain celibate in this way is a gift of grace, a charisma, that no one can seize of their own accord, but that those to whom it is given recognize as grace. It was given to Paul, and hence he could say, "I wish that all were as I myself am" (v. 7). At the same time he knew that each person receives his or her individual gift from God, and therefore "let each of you lead the life that the Lord has assigned, to which God called you" (v. 17). Any form of asceticism not derived from a vocation, a celibacy springing from any source other than the joy of the Holy Spirit, could bind a person to earthly cares more than marriage.

The church awaits the coming of her Lord and is on her way to meet her bridegroom. This fact may legitimately be reflected in people, in members of the church, who "made themselves eunuchs for the sake of the kingdom of heaven" (Matt 19:12). If Paul therefore can say, "It is well for a man not to touch a woman" (1 Cor 7:1), this does not contradict the Old Testament message that it is not good for a man to be alone (Gen 2:18). These individuals who remain single for the Lord's sake are not alone in the sense that they exist outside the sphere of human encounter. On the contrary, they stand within that encounter which all human encounters can only imitate; they stand in that relationship for which all "relationships" between husbands and wives are but a preparation. The Roman Catholic Church recognizes a "status of virginity." The ecclesiastical ceremony of the Dedication of a Virgin opens: "While preserving the blessing which rests on the holy condition of matrimony, it was nevertheless intended that there should be exalted souls who despise that physical sharing of their lives which is entered into by husband and wife . . . devoting all their love to that mystery which marriage faintly anticipates." We Protestants know no such "spiritual status," but perhaps, for all our protest against monasticism and a form of asceticism that had become in large measure a form of justification by works, we should not forget that the New Testament speaks of a celibacy that can be a "sign" of an ultimate bond, and therefore also a reminder to those who are married that "those who have wives be as though they had none" (1 Cor 7:29), and that Jesus himself said: "Whoever comes to me and does not hate father and mother, wife and children, brothers and sisters, yes, and even life itself, cannot be my disciple" (Luke 14:26).

This kind of celibacy may also perhaps become a light for those unmarried people who chafe at their condition as at an unwanted destiny. Gertrud von Le Fort comments aptly on this: "It becomes clear from Christ's *Sponsa* what the hidden significance of each virgin is, a significance defended unconsciously by even the unworthiest and least prepossessing of them." Life on one's own can avoid becoming the kind that is "not good" only if it can remain a life of encounter, that is, if it can be lived in the presence of God and one's fellow human beings. In other words, if properly understood, it is a life of service. It is appropriate to think at this point of the service rendered by widows (Acts 6:1; 1 Tim 5:5).

What, then, have we discovered about the position of women in the way of life of the new covenant? The most significant discovery, I suggest, is indeed this: that Jesus claims women for himself in the same way he does men, that he summons them out of their personal ties and places them in his service. A woman or wife, therefore, does not belong to the church of Jesus Christ in subjection to the man or to the husband, or through him; she is confronted directly with the Word of God. This equality — better thought of in terms of equal reprieve than of equal rights — highlights the limitation of all forms of earthly superiority and subjection. The command and the pattern of social order are not suspended by Jesus as such — the woman and the wife remain in their position of submission, but now this may and must be interpreted in the light of the central liberation experienced by women in their encounter with Jesus. A wife will then understand her encounter with her husband as a parable, and her position in this encounter as a copy of her position as a Christian in relation to the Lord — a position she now sees imbued with its special distinction and special responsibility. The restoration of their original partnership in Jesus Christ signifies for both husband and wife the summons to bear mutual witness to the grace they have received, the husband to the wife, the wife to the husband, and to display their ultimate unity precisely within their different roles. The way in which, as a result, sexual life is sanctified, however, serves to protect the dignity of the wife as a fellow human being in whom the husband recognizes his helper and partner.

Finally, the life of the single woman can be understood, in the light of the covenant of grace, as the qualified life of a human being who is "not alone" because of living in encounter, that is, of living with fellow human beings. Thus she can become an indication of the limitation of all earthly forms of order, and of their fulfillment in the kingdom of God.

# ❖ 3 ❖

# THE MINISTRY OF WOMEN IN THE
# PROCLAMATION OF THE WORD (I)

WHEN the Holy Spirit was poured out on the Day of Pentecost, Peter (Acts 2:16-18) extolled this event as the fulfillment of the prophecy of Joel (Joel 3:1-5 [NRSV 2:28-29]): "I will pour out my Spirit upon all flesh, and your sons and your daughters shall prophesy. . . . Even upon my slaves, both men and women, in those days I will pour out my Spirit; and they shall prophesy." No distinction is made here between men and women as recipients of the Holy Spirit. In the church of the new covenant, "everyone" is called and illumined by the Holy Spirit as a member of this church, and thus as a member of the body of Christ, and "everyone" is thus a recipient of the gifts of the Spirit (cf. Rom 13:1; 1 Cor 12:7; 11:18; Eph 4:7). Admittedly, the distribution of the gifts is various. "There are varieties of gifts, but the same Spirit" (1 Cor 12:4). The Spirit distributes them to each person as it wills. The variety of the gifts determines the variety of the forms of ministry within the church. Each form of ministry is necessary, and this means that no members of the church can elevate themselves above other members on the basis of the gifts they have received, and they certainly cannot despise others. For they are all members of one body (v. 12), and everyone needs everybody else: indeed, it is precisely the weakest who are needed most. In the New Testament we do not find any concept of office such as was later developed by the Roman Catholic Church, and such as we also find in

95

Lutheranism (e.g., in A. F. C. Vilmar). There is no priestly "profession" in the primitive church: the official priesthood of the old covenant, with its monopoly of access to the holy, has been abolished through the unique sacrifice of Jesus Christ. Now everyone who belongs to the church enjoys the same access to the Lord. They are all of them "taught by God" (1 Thess 4:9), they have all "received the Spirit" (Gal 6:1). "Now the office of preaching is not tied to any particular place or person, as the office of Levite was tied in the Law; rather, it is spread throughout the whole world and is to be found *where God distributes his gifts*" (Schmalkald Articles, 1538). The variety of forms of ministry, which rests on the variety of gifts, is under the control of the one Lord (1 Cor 12:5). Obedience in relation to him is the decisive criterion of each and every form of ministry.

This important chapter of 1 Corinthians does not mention different forms of ministry for men and for women. Men and women are in an identical fashion recipients of the Holy Spirit, and hence are in an identical fashion dependent on the bestowal of its gifts, and these gifts become manifest in them in an identical fashion for the benefit of the church, "for the common good" (v. 7).

We see from the book of Acts that women featured prominently in the history of the early mission of the church. From the outset it was women who were receptive to the Christian message, and hence from the outset the "sisters," *adelphai,* occupied an uncontested place in the emerging church (cf. Acts 1:14; 5:1; 6:1; 8:3; 9:2, 36; 12:12-13). Admittedly, whether these women participated in the proclamation of the Word is an issue about which opinion is divided (cf. Harnack, *Der Dienst der Frau in den ersten Jahrhunderten der christlichen Kirche* [The Ministry of Women During the First Centuries of the Christian Church] [Leipzig: 1902]). One can hardly have any doubt in the case of Priscilla, the wife of Aquila (Acts 18:2-3, 26). Both husband and wife appear together here in the church's missionary work. Paul describes them as those "who work with me" *(syn-*

*ergoi)* and sends greetings to them first (Rom 16:3). Priscilla is regularly named alongside Aquila, and the fact that she is generally (with the exception of 1 Cor 16:19) named first may be an indication of her importance in the church's work. Both of them together expounded "the Way of God" to Apollos (Acts 18:26). Harnack even went as far as to suggest that Priscilla may have been the author of Hebrews!

Two other women are named by Paul as his fellow workers: Euodia and Syntyche in Philippi. He says that they labored alongside him for the sake of the gospel, "together with Clement and the rest of my co-workers, whose names are in the book of life" (Phil 4:3). Admittedly, Ernst Lohmeyer (*Der Brief an die Philipper,* Meyer Kommentar [Göttingen: Vandenhoeck & Ruprecht, 1930], pp. 165-66) claims that what is being referred to here is confined to the situation of martyrdom, in other words that these two women were also involved in the church's suffering, whereas Harnack construes it more narrowly to refer to participation in the proclamation of the Word. It remains undisputed that in the early church more women than men were granted the gift of prophecy (Acts 21:9; 1 Cor 11:5-6).

Paul refers to *active participation* of women in worship. According to 1 Cor 11:5-6, women pray and prophesy at meetings of the Corinthian church. Although some have maintained that this reference is only to meetings of house churches, there is no basis for this in the text, and the claim is clearly contradicted by the link forward to the regulations regarding the Lord's Supper, which follow immediately after (1 Cor 11:17-18).[1] Paul appears to be familiar with women praying and prophesying in the congregation, that is, with women speaking with prophetic insight, and this seems to be regarded as perfectly

---

1. See E. Käsemann, "Die Frau in geistlichen Amt in der evangelischen Kirche" ("Women as Ministers in the Protestant Church") in *Protokoll für die Mitarbeiterinnen der evangelischen Frauenarbeit in Deutschland* (Minutes of the Workers of the Protestant Women's Guild in Germany). — Ed.

legitimate. According to our text the problem with which he is dealing does not concern the fact of this proclamation, but its manner. Both men and women pray and prophesy, but they should differ — not in the content of their proclamation! — in their . . . dress. The issue is an apparently minute one of outward appearance in church: men should minister bareheaded, but women with their heads covered. Yet according to Paul's argument at this point, this tiny issue determines whether the ministry is being carried out obediently. Moreover, the possibility of disobedience that Paul envisages and rejects here is without doubt that of women.

Why is Paul so passionately preoccupied with this issue of external appearance? Is he really so bound by custom that its rejection causes him this enormous concern? If that is the explanation, then one has to wonder why he made things so difficult for himself by introducing his admonition with the difficult notions of verse 3 instead of "omitting verse 3 together with the forced wordplay in verses 4-5 and relying in both cases simply on prevailing custom" (Hans Lietzmann, *An die Korinther I.II*, Handbuch zum Neuen Testament [Tübingen: Mohr, 1931], p. 53; and Wilhelm Bousset, *Schriften des Neuen Testaments* [Göttingen: Vandenhoeck & Ruprecht, 1917], p. 128). In order to understand why the apostle handles this question so insistently we must recall the situation of the Corinthian church. It was the first Christian church founded by Paul on the classical soil of ancient Greece, which was why Paul could say that he "became your father" (1 Cor 4:15) and why he regarded it as his dear child. Now in this position of paternal and apostolic authority he found himself under attack by the Corinthians, and in a twofold way: some acknowledged the first apostles as being superior to him, while others wanted to free the church altogether from apostolic authority of any kind and put themselves directly under the Lord's command. Adolf Schlatter even goes so far as to claim (*Paulus, der Bote Jesu* [Paul, Messenger of Jesus] [Stuttgart: Calwer, 1934], p. 5) that the epistle has "only one

98

theme," namely, "justifying the apostle's authority, which the church cannot evade."

The church at Corinth was a church richly endowed with gifts of the Spirit. Paul can tell them that he gives thanks to God always concerning them because of the grace of God which was given to them and in which "in every way you have been enriched in him" (1:4-5). Yet this very wealth turns into a temptation for the church. It runs the risk of an enthusiastic, and by the same token erroneous, understanding of Christian freedom. And here the apostle begins to adopt a contradictory position. The church is not to abandon its subjection, is not to seek to reign and become rich "without us," is not to reckon itself "higher" than is written in Scripture (4:6-7). "Be imitators of me," Paul cries to them, after depicting his life as an apostle as a life of suffering, and one lived beneath a cross (4:16). "Be imitators of me, as I am of Christ," reads the first verse of the chapter that concerns us particularly (11:1). What also matters is for the church to remain faithful to the crucified Lord, and hence to the *paradosis,* the tradition delivered to them, which has its origin in him. He, who delivered himself up that they might live, wants them to bear witness to him. The church is nourished and "built up" by witnessing to the crucified and resurrected Lord. Schlier is surely correct to say that the Corinthian church was an "enthusiastic church," which "not only in practice lived to a considerable extent with an almost tangible sense of the life of the Spirit, but understood this to be above all what Christian living meant," and that therefore "building up" this church had to mean recalling it "to the church of tangible, biblical, signs of the End" (*Evangelische Theologie* 8 [1948/49] 463). "All things are lawful for me, but not all things are beneficial . . . not all things build up" (6:12; 10:23).

This tension between Christian freedom and the obedience that consists in emulation — or as Schlier says, between revelation and love — permeates the whole letter. In practical terms the church's obedience is to be shown in obedience to the

99

apostle. "I commend you because you remember me in everything and maintain the traditions just as I handed them on to you" (11:2). If we take up the notion of "tradition" here in all the fullness of meaning hinted at earlier, then nobody will be inclined to construe it as meaning "customs." What is at issue here is a decision of obedience, the completion of Christian life in knowledge of the crucified Lord. Subordination of the church to this Lord, and thus to his envoy, the apostle Paul, is reflected in the subordination of women in relation to men. Paul speaks of the relation of men to women in this text, explicitly drawing a parallel with the respective positions of the superiority and subordination of Jesus Christ himself. The members of the church in Corinth are to know that this earthly relation is a copy and a parable, pointing in the direction of the Lord of all relations and patterns of order. That is why Paul anchors the anthropological saying "the man is the head of the woman" [NRSV margin] between two christological sayings, "Christ is the head of every man" and "God is the head of Christ." Christ is Lord, and as such the head of all principality *(archē)* and power *(exousia)* (Col 2:10).

Within the framework of earthly order, man, in contrast to woman, is the bearer of power. He is designated the "head," and as noted previously, what this means in New Testament terms is that the person so designated is, within any given order of creation, the superordinate, ruling partner and representative of order as such. This earthly bearer of power, the man, is confronted by the apostle with the Lord who has "power over all," and whose power is therefore the foundation and limitation of all other power. The Christian man must know that as an earthly power he is subject to this heavenly "head." Christ is the head of all men, whether they know it or not. Yet the only man who truly knows his task and destiny as a man is he who knows and acknowledges this heavenly "head."

The exalted Lord, however, is he who abased himself — the resurrected Lord is the crucified Lord. When the apostle says in

1 Cor 11:3 that "God is the head of Christ," he means this to indicate that Jesus Christ has rendered the obedience that was unto death, subjecting himself in this voluntary act of love as the everlasting Son to the everlasting Father (15:28). Thus he, the Lord to whom everything is subject and who therefore exists in unqualified superiority, is at the same time the very essence of subjection. Thus he justifies and relativizes the position of man and the position of woman. Within the framework of earthly order woman stands over against man in obedience, that is, within this framework she is the subordinate partner, determined by the other. In the apostle's eyes this position is certainly no less valuable and no more disadvantaged a position: it is Christ's position in relation to the Father; it is his, the apostle's — and the church's — place in relation to the Lord. It would be an egregious error to see in this verse 3 a "hierarchy," and to overlook the distinct break introduced by Paul between the christological and the anthropological sayings. It would be to confuse reality and its model, and sadly this has happened repeatedly in exegeses of this verse. This would necessarily deprive women of a direct link to Christ — as indeed Schlatter does (*Paulus*, p. 30) — and to relegate them to a position that they would *have to* rebel against. The apostle wanted to avoid any such monstrous implication, as is apparent from verse 3c. On the one hand, Christ as the model of all obedience and subjection bears witness to the obedience of women and their position of subjection; on the other hand, as exalted Lord and the head of all power and dominion, he determines the higher position of men. It is true: man is the head of woman; but it is true within this crucially important set of brackets that transforms everything. Christians should know this.

The church in Corinth needs to be told this by the apostle. It needs to be reminded of its position in relation to its Lord and his representative, the apostle. The conduct of the church is reflected in the conduct of the church's women, and it is they who therefore acquire particular significance here. Their natural position as women gives them a special responsibility. If they fail in this, then they withhold from the church the particular power of witnessing invested in them precisely as women, which consists of them being, in their natural subjection, a pointer toward the subjection that the church owes its Lord. The members of the church in Corinth stand in danger of taking it for granted, in their enthusiasm, that they could consider the richness of the experiences they had been blessed with to be an occasion for boasting, and "puffing themselves up," and deciding for themselves in whose hands the leadership of the church should lie. This means, however, that they are in danger of "lording it" where they should serve, and of refusing obedience to the apostle and, in him, the Lord who had sent him.

This ominous error by the church could also be seen in the fact that the Christian women in Corinth appeared to think that, in the new era of freedom, differences of sex were irrelevant. And since they could receive the Holy Spirit and its gifts just like men, and since, therefore, they were honored with the same revelation, they were now absolved of their position of subjection. This led to a disastrous tendency to abandon marriage or indeed to spiritualize it, but it was also significant for the ministry of women in the church. Clearly, women no longer wanted to wear the symbol of their position as women — the veil covering their hair — while exercising their functions during church services, believing that this symbol was superfluous in view of the distinction between men and women in the church having been cancelled out.

Paul rejects this view, and does so astonishingly sharply. Just as it would be a disgrace if the men sought to wear such head covering, similarly it would be a disgrace if the women sought to pray and speak bareheaded. On the one hand, the man, who is the head of the woman, and at the same time subject to the heavenly head, dishonors both himself and his Lord, thus disgracing his head in two senses of the term, if he seeks to wear the "symbol" that befits the woman. It amounts to a denial of his position and responsibility as a man, and a transgression against the pattern of order that he has been charged to uphold. On the other hand, the woman dishonors her head if she bares it while praying and prophesying during a church service, thereby denying her position as a woman, disgracing both herself and the man, and transgressing against the pattern of order in which they have been placed. "It is one and the same thing as having her head shaved," says Paul, meaning: as if she lived a disorderly life, in a man-woman partnership that had been destroyed or indeed perverted. (According to Lietzmann the shaving of the head was at that time the mark of a prostitute; Dellings says, especially for a perverted prostitute; while others declare shaving to have been the punishment for adulteresses.)

The fact of man being the head of the woman is still, and indeed especially, valid within the church. If it were to become irrelevant here, this would mean that it had been an inconsequential and purely provisional matter. But it is not. Only fanatical enthusiasts could conclude that earthly forms of law and order were no longer binding on Christians — on the contrary, it is to Christians that their true meaning first becomes apparent.

"For a man ought not to have his head veiled, since he is the image and glory [NRSV margin] of God; but woman is the glory [NRSV margin] of man," continues Paul (1 Cor 11:7), referring to the order of things established at the creation of man and woman. "Indeed, man was not made from woman, but woman from man" (v. 8). (J. J. Bachofen comments that with this observation Paul stands opposed in principle to mythological thought and its Orphic principle that moved from the bottom up, from the mother to the father! *Myth, Religion, and Mother Right,* trans. Ralph Manheim, Bollingen Series 84 [Princeton: Princeton University Press, 1967], p. 112.) "Neither was man created for the sake of woman, but woman for the sake of man" (v. 9). That the man is the head of the woman is not, therefore, an order of things determined by sin, but that was his position

103

"from the beginning," just as the woman is assigned to him "from the beginning" as his "helper" and companion. Thus as the head of the woman the man is destined to be the image and glory of God — not apart from her, then, but "from the beginning" only *with* her. Over man without woman there hangs the judgment: "It is not good that the man should be alone" (Gen 2:18), and the reason why this is so is precisely because it is only in the appropriate form of encounter with his fellow human being that he encounters his Creator. In the encounter with this fellow human being, the woman, the man recognizes himself as the one who is "not alone" but lives in relationship, thereby becoming prepared for relationship with God. Woman is the "helper" whom he needs and in the creating of whom God completes the creation of humankind. Thus she is the glory of man, as he is intended, as her head, to be the glory of God.

Paul tells us in which man this intention, an intention harmonized with creation, is fulfilled: in the "last Adam," in the "new man," in Jesus Christ as the head of his church (2 Cor 4:4, 6; and Col 2:15). He is the image and glory of God to whom the earthly man as the head of the woman can never do more than point. Again and again, though, he must become this point of reference, imitating or reflecting the glory of God that rests on this heavenly head, and thus becoming himself its "reflection" (thus Schlier in *Theological Dictionary of the New Testament,* trans. and ed. Geoffrey W. Bromiley [Grand Rapids: Eerdmans, 1965], s.v. *kephalē,* 3:679), while woman must become the image of the church, thereby becoming the glory of the man as the church is the glory of Christ. What counts in the man-woman relationship is for the woman, who was "from the beginning," to be disclosed in the light of the covenant of grace in her true and ultimate meaning.

"The man is the head of the woman." That is not a saying that loses its significance in the context of Christian freedom; rather, only in the church does it first acquire its true importance. If the women of Corinth were to do away with the "symbol" of their position as women in relation to men when they minister to the congregation, they would thereby proclaim their ignorance of their position, and flout it in an erroneous understanding of Christian freedom. At the same time, they would be depriving the church of the particular role as direction finders that is bound up with their lives as women, and would run the risk of lacking credibility in their witness, even if their praying and speaking were charismatic praying and speaking. Instead of being the glory of the man, they would be dishonoring their "heads." ("She brings dishonor on all men," says Calvin at this point.)

"For this reason the woman ought to have a symbol of authority [*exousia*] on her head, because of the angels" (v. 10). It is not clear how the notion of *exousia* should be translated here. Basically, though, commentators agree that what is meant is a "symbol" of the *power* to which the woman is subject. Gerhard Kittel argues that *exousia* goes back to an Aramaic word with a proved meaning, in one place where it occurs, of "veil," and that the Greek word rests on an error in translation.[2] Yet even this interpretation does not force any basic change in my line of argument, for on this view too the passage is about the "symbol" that the woman may not dispense with during worship. Recently Stephan Losch has suggested (*Theologische Quartalschrift* 44 [1947] 215-61) a new "attempt at a solution": Paul was seeking to prevent the intrusion of a gentile ritual custom. The issue was one of gentile Christian women who until recently had been taking part in sacrifices and processions in honor of their local deities, and always with their hair loose.

The meaning of the clause "because of the angels" is also difficult. Following Tertullian, some have suggested a parallel in Gen 6:1, where the "sons of God" lusted after the beauty of the daughters of men, and similarly the angels might be led into temptation by the uncovered hair of women. However, this train

2. Kittel, *Rabbinica* (1920), pp. 17-31. — Ed.

of thought does not fit in with the text — quite apart from the questionable exegesis of Gen 6:1-2 that is involved! In the whole passage Paul is clearly concerned with the man-woman relation and the symbol of that relationship. It is therefore more natural to see in the "angels" the representatives of the heavenly order proclaiming the divine claim to power over the earthly realm too. Any denial of the earthly order would affect this divine claim to power. Hence the angels are disturbed if there is any damage to the earthly order. The interpretation given by Schlier (*Dictionary*, 3:679-80) is surely significant too, that the angels are the representatives of the presence of God and Christ in the church's worship. Bousset presents a similar view, while adding that both in the church's collective worship and in individual prayer the angels are present as mediators between God and humanity, bearing the prayers of the faithful up to God's throne (so too Schlatter, *Paulus,* pp. 312-13). In any event, Paul intends the phrase "because of the angels" to mean that woman's disobedience not only occurs in the eyes of the earthly church but is also seen by the heavenly world. Thus he bestows cosmic significance on an event that is apparently nothing more than a trivial matter of external appearance. If on the one hand the realm of the "angels" is entered, on the other hand the realm of the demons emerges. The woman who fails to cover her head in church, and thereby makes it plain that, from an erroneous understanding of Christian freedom, she regards the proper order operative between man and woman to be irrelevant within the church, does something "dishonorable," thus opening the doors to the powers of chaos as the adversaries of God's proper order.

"Nevertheless, in the Lord woman is not independent of man or man independent of woman. For just as woman came from man, so man comes through woman; but all things come from God" (vv. 11-12). For all this passionate pleading on behalf of the natural order, and for its being upheld within the church too, Paul is nevertheless aware of its limitations: he is aware of the Lord of all order. In him the man-woman relation is a relation

106

of complete equality. "If anyone is in Christ, there is a new creation" [2 Cor 5:17]. When Paul writes to the church in Corinth that the man is the head of the woman, he is talking about this "new creation." Here all traces of superiority on the part of the man are excluded, and therefore any protest on the part of the woman is unnecessary. Here man and woman know themselves to be one, and in their mutual complementarity they attest the goodness of God's order. Here woman is aware that, as the one taken from man's body, she would negate her own existence if she were to try to separate herself from it, and here man is aware that, as the one who has come from woman, he can only appear before God *with* this fellow human being. Thus it becomes clear that the order established at creation is not a contingent matter that is of no significance among Christians, but rather that it is precisely in the Lord, that is, in his church, that it can be recognized as the gracious order of God, and is to be attested as such.

From this perspective it becomes impossible for the woman to be able to think of removing the symbol of her position as woman during worship. And Paul is in a position, after all his arguments, to appeal to the judgment of the church: "Judge for yourselves: is it proper for a woman to pray to God with her head unveiled?" He can even refer to the long hair given by *nature* as a "covering" (1 Cor 11:13-15)! If one understands just what it is that the symbol symbolizes, one is in a position to grasp the true meaning of this "natural" gift. Paul is not engaging here in "natural theology," but acknowledging nature in the service of revelation.

The whole question of the covering or veiling of women is for Paul an agreement that the churches have entered into, nothing more and nothing less (v. 16). Only the dissent of the women in the church at Corinth gives this matter such importance as an issue of obedience that Paul has to handle it with this degree of urgency because it becomes for him symptomatic of the Corinthian church's tendency to high-handedness, which leads them to risk falling away from the tradition in their erroneous understanding of Christian freedom.

Two chapters later Paul returns to the behavior of women in the church. "As in all the churches of the saints, women should be silent in the churches. For they are not permitted to speak, but should be subordinate, as the law also says. If there is anything they desire to know, let them ask their husbands at home. For it is shameful for a woman to speak in church" (14:33-35).

What is happening here? In the same situation, and addressing the same audience, Paul writes these sentences in the same letter, even though they appear so obviously to contradict what he was saying to the Corinthians in chapter 11. There he refers to women praying and prophesying in public in the congregation and raises no objection to this procedure in principle, whereas here he commands women to keep silent in the churches. The simplest solution to this difficulty, and one that has been suggested many times before, is to take this passage to be a later interpolation linked to 1 Tim 2:11. Alternatively, one can interpret 1 Corinthians 11 as referring only to services taking place in "house churches," whereas here [in chap. 14] it is the full assembly of the whole church that is being referred to — though as noted earlier, there is no textual basis for this (cf. Lietzmann, *An die Korinther,* p. 75). Or again, one can resort to inferring that the speaking *(lalein)* referred to here is different from the prophesying — prophetic speaking — in chapter 11, and conclude, therefore, that Paul is concerned to ban only uncharismatic teaching. Yet according to chapter 12, "teaching" is also a gift of grace, and there is no speaking in church that is anything other than speaking in the Spirit. Hence — since the women in the church are also recipients of the Holy Spirit — one simply has to face up to the difficulty that Paul is here demanding an end to the gifts of the Spirit, just as immediately beforehand he declares that anyone speaking in tongues should keep silent in church if no interpreter is present (14:28), and prophets should take turns to speak, for "the spirits of prophets are subject to the prophets" (v. 32). We are left, therefore, as Lietzmann says, "with a contradiction" between 11:5-6 and 14:34-35, although of course I cannot accept his further opinion that in chapter 11 Paul allows "praying" and "prophesying" to women only "reluctantly," demands the veil or head covering unconditionally, and now discloses his true opinion: "women shall keep silent altogether" (*An die Korinther*, p. 75). Let us rather consider whether we cannot achieve an altogether more satisfying outcome than hitherto simply by holding these two passages in tension without trying to harmonize them.

Paul speaks in 1 Corinthians 14 of the order of service. It appears that, in Corinth, speaking in tongues had got out of hand. On the one hand, Paul has no hesitation in acknowledging it as a gift of the Holy Spirit, while insisting on the other hand that as part of public worship it needs to be restrained because of its unintelligibility. Those who speak in tongues "build up" themselves, whereas those who prophesy build up the whole congregation. And that is the goal of all proclamation: the building up of the church (v. 26), that is, the growth of the body of Christ. It is the Lord himself who builds up his church, and all human proclamation can only be a witness to this act of Christ. The witness must take place, however, within a particular framework of order; it must be heard and understood in order to prompt and promote faith in all those who hear and understand. Hence the apostle rejects "unintelligible" speaking in tongues in church, as well as the practice of everyone speaking at the same time. What is important is not for each individual to indulge in an uninhibited display of the gift they have received, even though there is no doubt about its authenticity as a gift of grace from the Holy Spirit, but for them to allow themselves to be guided in its exercise by the aim of all proclamation, namely, that it should be used to *serve* the Lord of all gifts, and hence too his church. The church in Corinth was rich in gifts and thus also rich in insight. The apostle is not trying to deny them this wealth.

He thanks God for it. Yet he seems to feel obliged to tell this living, richly endowed church that there is something "better" than all forms of wealth, and that is the love that "builds up," that "edifies." Without this love all gifts and all insight "are worthless." He speaks of the love that never ceases, he speaks of the love of Jesus Christ, from and in which his church lives. He chose them in this love and he preserves them in this love. As people loved by him in this way, his followers may also love each other and serve each other.

We should not forget that Paul, in this letter, after speaking of the gifts of the Spirit, speaks of this love (ch. 13), by which he certainly does not mean any kind of sentimentality, but the very lifeblood of the church, which is the body of the Lord. He has this love in mind when he is talking about the order of service to be adhered to during congregational worship, an order of service that is wholly intended for the purpose of building up the church. It is in this connection that he commands women to remain silent in church. "Paul addresses some women who are not keeping in their place," observes Franz-J. Leenhardt (*La place de la Femme,* p. 37), but it is implausible to construe this command to be silent as having been evoked by some special pushiness on the part of the Corinthian women in particular, because Paul says explicitly, "as in all the churches of the saints" (v. 33). On the contrary, what we have here is a command that is very basic in character. Women endowed with gifts of the Spirit — and there is no question but that, as members of the church, they are recipients of the Holy Spirit and hence too of its gifts, just as the men are — should not exercise their gifts, should not "speak" in church, but should . . . be subject. "If there is anything they desire to 'learn' [NRSV 'know'], let them ask their husbands at home. For it is shameful for a woman to speak in church" (v. 35). This verse has been used to support the conclusion that the ban on speaking applies only to married women, and that chapter 11 therefore applies to unmarried women, who are permitted to pray aloud and prophesy in church. The text

110

offers no support for this conclusion, however, because "their husbands" could be translated "their menfolk" and refer to a father or brother. The apostle does not regard it as permissible to break the silence in church because of a "desire to know." Cf. 1 Tim 2:11. Moreover, the notion of "learning" indicates that the woman, even though she does not speak, does possess insight.

In 1 Cor 14:35c the apostle declares that it is "shameful" for a woman to speak during congregational worship, in the same sense that in 11:5 he said that she would be "disgracing" or "dishonoring" her head if she left it uncovered. On both occasions what is at issue is not custom but a decision motivated by obedience.

It is, then, a form of service, of ministry, that is being demanded of women, namely, that of submission, and of signaling this by their silence in church. This form of ministry appears to the apostle to be eminently important; for what is at stake is a form of ministry that will "build up" the church. It would be a mistake to see in this demand an unfriendly gesture on the part of the apostle. Rather, one should note the positive emphasis given by Paul to this silence of women in church, construed as a sign of their subjection. This will be possible, however, only if one sees this sign in the context of the early Christian church, whose pattern of worship displayed a very different structure from that of the modern church service.

The first Christians gathered daily in the temple (Acts 2:46; 5:42) or in private houses (1 Cor 16:19). In the book of Acts we find teaching, preaching, prayer, and the breaking of bread as the main features of these gatherings (2:42, 46; 20:7), while the picture we find in Paul (1 Corinthians 12) is still fuller. The climax is the meal celebrated in commemoration of the meals shared by the risen Lord with his disciples, and celebrated as an announcement of the forthcoming messianic banquet. Contrary to traditional opinion, Oscar Cullmann does not regard a separation of preaching and Eucharist as characteristic of early Chris-

111

tianity (*Early Christian Worship*, trans. A. S. Todd and J. B. Torrance, Studies in Biblical Theology 1/10 [Naperville: Allenson, 1953]). He argues that there were *two* parts of *one* church service (Acts 2:42; 20:7-8). Baptism, by contrast — as befitted its unique character — constituted a particular act of worship, so that (according to Cullmann) the church's worship in early Christianity consisted of two forms of celebration: the common meal together with preaching, and baptism.

It is this characteristic of congregational worship that one must bear in mind when trying to understand the apostle's instruction that women should be silent during services. This silence on the part of women is not some kind of dead point within the active life of worship; rather it is a necessary function. It operates — as does all speaking out loud during worship — in the knowledge of the Holy Spirit and, therefore, like speaking out loud, it "builds up," it "edifies" the church. This silence points to the limitation of all human speech, and designates the area of "need of only one thing" that Jesus attributes to Mary (Luke 10:42). The silent women represent the listening church — which the teaching church must constantly revert to being. It is the silence of respect in the risen Lord, of the Lord of the church. That it should be the women who are both obliged and permitted to perform this particular service follows from the parabolic character of their natural position. "And you, O woman, for you it is indeed reserved to be able to be the image of the hearer and reader of the Word who is not forgetful. . . . Nature certainly has not been unfair to you woman, nor has Christianity either" (Søren Kierkegaard, *For Self-Examination* and *Judge for Yourselves*, ed. and trans. Howard V. Hong and Edna H. Hong [Princeton: Princeton University Press, 1990], pp. 46, 48). Women, by their silence, proclaim their subjection, thereby reminding the church that it is the earthly church of the heavenly Lord and needs to remain mindful of his death, and that means of the cross. They restrain it from any form of untoward fanaticism or ecstasy.

The shape that our church services take today no longer leaves room for this "sign." In a gathering in which men too are silent, with one exception, and in which there is so little trace of "enthusiasm," silence on the part of women can no longer have the same meaning. In addition, in a form of church service whose focus has been reduced so drastically to the proclamation of the word, their silence loses the significance it acquired, in the early Christian church, from the Lord's Supper, at which the presence of the Lord was celebrated. Men and women alike participated equally in their meal, and it was here that the women who were silent in church were ultimately compelled, but therefore also permitted, to be silent. This pivotal point of the whole service sustained all forms of service or ministry. If, today, one were to try to infer from this Pauline command to women that they should be silent in all circumstances, and that therefore they were to be denied the opportunity of proclaiming the Word, one would be taking what for Paul was a living and concrete context, and one that was only intelligible as such, and turning it into a rigid general rule. How far this was from Paul's intention can be seen from the fact that he can speak in the same letter of a woman speaking in church (11:5) without calling this in question, provided that she does not deny her position as a woman.

The question that arises for women, and particularly for women theologians, from these two passages, and one that calls for careful scrutiny, is whether in their preaching and proclamation they perform a service that "builds up," "edifies," the church and whether in so doing they are imbued with the love that is greater than all gifts. That also needs to be the question asked by every man who proclaims the Word. Women, however, learn from Paul that this question is asked of them in a particular form, namely, whether by undertaking these responsibilities they do not depart from the position of subjection required of them. On the one hand, the "battle for the pulpit" has unfortunately all too often been conducted by women too as a battle for their "rights," thereby forfeiting the credibility it could otherwise have

113

if their concern centered on "building up" the church. On the other hand, admittedly, those women who remain silent in church must face up to the question of whether their silence is a silence in the Holy Spirit, and thus in revelation and love, rather than quite simply the inertia and thoughtlessness of a custom that prevents women in particular from issuing a lively summons to a fresh restructuring of our church services today.

Here, though, we find yet another passage in the New Testament that is quoted to prevent women from proclaiming the Word — 1 Tim 2:8ff. This passage presents a particular challenge because we appear to be faced with the simple choice of sacrificing either women or the text of the epistle. Leenhardt has opted for the latter. "It seems to us futile to search for conciliation with the letter to the Corinthians. A different spirit animates these pages. Where is it blowing from? It is of little consequence whether it is Jewish or clericalist or dualist. It appears to be neither biblical nor from the gospel" (*La place de la Femme*, p. 44). This bald statement — favoring women! — compels us all the more urgently to allow the text to speak to us.

The second chapter of 1 Timothy deals with prayer in church. After exhorting the whole church to offer up prayers, intercessions, and thanksgivings on behalf of all people, for kings and all that occupy high positions, Paul directs: "in every place the men should pray, lifting up holy hands without anger or argument" [v. 8]. Calvin's view is that this refers to disputes in the church between Jewish and gentile Christians (Corpus Reformatum, 53:190). Women, however, are told (vv. 9-10), that they should "pray [Greek/NRSV 'dress themselves'] modestly and decently in suitable clothing, not with their hair braided, or with gold, pearls, or expensive clothes, but with good works, as is proper for women who profess reverence for God." Like men, women are called on to pray in church, and like them they have access to their Father in heaven through the one mediator, Jesus Christ. The woman who prays has no need to better her position or vie for approval by adorning herself. She must make no efforts to impress the people around her. She is in the best position imaginable as the child of him whom she can address as "Our Father." Her adornment will therefore be the "inner self with the lasting beauty of a gentle and quiet spirit" (1 Pet 3:4). "He has given us Jesus Christ for our apparel," comments Calvin on this passage. Thus adorned, she will be "modest and sensible" and do good works, that is, she will bear witness to the favor that has befallen her, and so will perform works of gratitude, thereby glorifying God. And *learn* in the silence, for she is called like the man to the knowledge of the truth (1 Tim 2:4). "We are all disciples of God. . . . Because if we are babies he must make us listen to the voice of our shepherd. That applies not only to women, that they may learn; men must also have their part" (ibid., 280).

That women must learn "in silence" *(en hesychia)* does not mean merely, say, that they should be silent, but has the broader meaning that they are in that position of security in which they too — and they especially — stand above the (by worldly standards) vulnerable position of subordinate. Not for nothing does woman appear in the framework of the "household codes" in the same list as the servant and the child, in other words, in a list of "weaker" people. This need not become for her any cause for disquiet if she acknowledges, with the gratitude of a creature who has found peace before her Creator, that she has been put into this position by God, and further acknowledges — from a spiritual perspective — the special distinction of this position in particular.

Now it would appear that in the church at Ephesus, to which 1 Timothy is addressed, some women could not reconcile their position with Christian freedom, and rebelled against the subjection demanded of them. They pushed their way into the "teaching office," and clearly sought to gain predominance over men in doing so. For the writer of the letter declares: "I permit no woman to teach or to have authority over a man; she is to keep silent" (2:12). According to 1 Cor 14:26, teaching, *didas-*

115

*kalia,* was a gift of the Holy Spirit, and could, therefore, like all charismata, be given to women. Yet now this form of ministry is highlighted by being connected with the notion of *autenthein andros,* of having dominion over a man. Adolf Schlatter argues, admittedly, that it belongs to the very nature of a teacher to have dominion. "The woman teaching would have dominion over the man, and that is something Paul refuses her permission to do" (*Die kirche der Griechen im Urteil des Paulus* [The Church of the Greeks in the Judgment of Paul] [Stuttgart: Calwer, 1936], p. 89). However, there appears to have been a particular tendency toward arrogance on the part of the women at Ephesus, for the writer to block their path so brusquely and feel obliged to remind them (vv. 13-14) of their creation and fall, in connection with which the fateful prominence assumed by Eve surely does not betoken either a cause or a greater degree of sin, but does disclose that, with the entry of sin, the established order in which man and woman had been arranged by God at creation was perverted. Both fell, and therefore both, man and woman together, are dependent on redemption. Even the judgment that God imposed on Eve, "In pain you shall bring forth children, yet your desire shall be for your husband, and he shall rule over you" (Gen 3:16), will not be the final word. Indeed, already in this word of judgment there shines forth the promise: Adam calls his wife "Eve," mother of the living — Israel's hope rests on her children.

Now it would appear that the Christian women at Ephesus, following the birth of *the* child, no longer regarded conceiving and giving birth to children as "in keeping with the times," and rebelled against this natural destiny of woman. Our text tells them that the only thing that matters is their salvation, and that this can happen even when they are quite simply mothers, "provided they continue in faith and love and holiness, with modesty" [1 Tim 2:15]. It would be a mistake, therefore, to claim that the writer is referring here to *teknogonia,* to childbearing, as *the* work demanded of them. For one would then need to ask with Joachim

116

Jeremias whether this was not a case of "salvation" through "works," and whether in this passage we were not already catching a glimpse of "a bit of early Catholicism" (*Die Briefe an Timotheus und Titus,* 7th ed., Das Neue Testament Deutsch 9 [Göttingen: Vandenhoeck & Ruprecht, 1954], p. 16). "Saint Paul did not wish to establish here some merits as if he said that the cause of our salvation came from good works, that the women saved themselves when they applied themselves to do what they had to do" (Calvin, Corpus Reformatum, 53:232). Nor should we emphasize the "healthy bourgeois ethic of the Pastoral Epistles," as urged by Martin Dibelius (*Pastoralbriefe,* Handbuch zum Neuen Testament [Tübingen: Mohr (Siebeck), 1931], p. 31). What is far more to the point is that women's salvation from judgment and through judgment is being proclaimed to them here. The expression that is used here, *sōzesthai dia tinos,* appears at only one other place in the New Testament, and there it means: "to be saved through something" (see 1 Cor 3:15: "he himself shall be saved but only as through fire"; see K. von Hofmann, *Die erster Briefe an die Korinther,* Die heilige Schrift des Neuen Testaments 6 [1874], pp. 103, 187). "I was appointed a herald and an apostle," says the author in verse 7. And women may hold fast to this proclamation irrespective of which vocation they follow. For then they live in faith and in love and in sanctification with discipline. A lack of discipline, however much it may be justified by appeals to spirituality, betrays a lack of Christian insight. Yet it is just such a lack of discipline that the writer must have perceived in these women's desire to engage in teaching. He recalls them to their proper situation, where they can be assured of their salvation precisely by submitting to this situation. Let us remember once again that all this is being said in the context of prayer in church.

Understood in this way, it seems disconcerting to reproach the text for being neither biblical nor Protestant, and also the reference to the Fall can hardly be designated an "error of taste" or an "error of theology" or even as "lacking in gallantry"

(Leenhardt, *La place de la Femme*, pp. 41-42), even if parallels can be drawn with a Jewish line of argument, parallels that nevertheless in the context of the train of thought as a whole take on a very different meaning. This passage, 1 Tim 2:11-15, cannot be used either, then, in support of the view that the apostle intended to establish a law that would ban women from the ministry of "teaching" forevermore. On the contrary, and quite in accordance with the passages we looked at from 1 Corinthians, it can only be intended to remind women that their ministry in proclaiming the Word will serve to build up the church and will be legitimate only when it is necessary for just this purpose. Certainly this same demand applies equally to men who wish to speak in church, but it applies more sharply to women because their primary form of ministry in all circumstances is to allow their position as women to resonate with its particular aptness as a lived parable. This is not in any sense a demotion of women — on the contrary, it is a form of ministry that is especially important in the church. What the "sign" or "symbol" may be today for women's subordination to men in the church's worship is something that will become apparent only from listening carefully to the whole of Scripture, and certainly not by a legalistic use of isolated passages, which is alien to Scripture itself, and serves, not the proclamation of the living Lord, but all too human "prejudices." The latter, even if expressed in a tone of utter conviction by Lutheran and Reformed pastors, cannot help one iota and will indeed only deepen the confusion. Thus when, for example, today(!) a Reformed clergyman in Germany decrees: "Women should hear the Word of God from the mouth of men. That is their lot in view of the Fall" (*Das Wort und die Zeit* no. 4, 15.4.49, "Die Frau in der Gemeinde"), one may be forgiven for asking whether there has not been some mix-up between the apostle (naturally, both women *and* men should hear the Word of God from *this* man's mouth!) and a clergyman and theologian who is, when all is said and done, not an apostle!

Yet if the men theologians leave us so very much in the lurch on this issue, then we women must not respond by having recourse to false lines of argument ourselves, but must truly think and speak — hopefully more appositely than hitherto — from the absolutely basic perspective of the forms of ministry and service that will contribute to the building of the church, and take seriously as our partners in dialogue all men who think and speak on the basis of this same perspective. A most welcome contribution in this respect is the astonishingly enlightened one made by the Anglican Canon R. W. Howard in three sermons delivered at the University of Oxford: *Should Women Be Priests?* (Oxford: Basil Blackwell, 1949).

## ❖ 4 ❖

# THE "MOTHER OF ALL LIVING"

ONE central area of a woman's life has not yet been broached
in our discussions, that of motherhood. It is the testimony of
the Old Testament in particular that we need to take into account
here.

The word of judgment that God utters to woman after the
Fall refers to her motherhood:

> I will greatly increase your pangs in childbearing.
> in pain you shall bring forth children;
> yet your desire shall be for your husband,
> and he shall rule over you. (Gen 3:16)

Here the central theme is no longer the dipolarity between man
and woman; instead, woman is addressed in the role of mother.
Man and woman appear here to be honored only in respect of
offspring, and their direct relationship to be transformed into a
shared orientation toward children. Only in woman's desire does
there peep through some sense of it not having been thus from
the beginning. She seeks man, her man, and finds in him her
master. In contrast with the position envisaged for her at creation,
her position as found in historical activity is a vulnerable one:
she is no longer an equal helper, but an item of property subordinate to man, who governs her. He no longer calls her *ishshah*,

the person taken from man, but "Eve," the "mother of all living." Still, by giving her this name he indicates that even in the new situation he hopes for her assistance, namely, her assistance as mother.

The biblical writer of this account comes from Israel. His perception of the relation of man and woman was that man was the master of woman, the *baal*, while woman was the property, the *beulah*, of man, gained originally in robbery, later by payment, and later still accompanied by a so-called dowry from her family and kin. He knew the strict laws by which the Israelite man defended his property: there was the death penalty for adultery, both for the adulterer and for the adulterous wife (Deut 22:22; cf. Exod 16:40 and John 8:5-7). The husband could own several wives, and he could divorce a wife if he found something "shameful" in her, that is, according to Deut 22:20 and 24:1, if he found her not to be a virgin. In Judaism this notion of "shamefulness" was broadened until eventually it included everything displeasing to the husband.

By contrast, the woman could not dissolve the marriage. If the husband were to die, she transferred with her inheritance to his nearest male relation. If he left her childless, his brother had to plant seed in his widow so that the name of the deceased did not disappear in Israel, and so that the land should be kept in the line of descent (Gen 38:12-13; Deut 26:1-10; Ruth 3–4; cf. also Matt 22:23-24). Only when the wife became a mother and bore a son did she truly become a member of the husband's kin, and gain an honorable place there. To her children she is someone to be respected like their father (Exod 20:12; Deut 15:16), and some laws even mention her before the father (Lev 19:3; 21:2). Whoever curses their mother is liable to the same punishment as the person who curses their father, namely, the death penalty (Exod 21:17; Deut 20:19; cf. also Deut 27:16). The mother also has the right of chastisement (Deut 21:16-17). In respect of servants she has a position of domination too (Gen 16:6). In the royal family of Israel, she occupies a particularly honorable place:

she is called a mistress and presides over the royal women's quarters (1 Kgs 2:13; 15:13; 2 Kgs 10:13; Isaiah 13, 18, 29). Where the lengths of various kings' reigns are recorded, the mothers of the kings of Judah are always named (cf. 1 Kings 14, 21, 15, etc.).

The hidden background to the importance thus attached to descendants, and hence to the mother, was hope for the fulfillment of the promise made by God to the patriarchs and later encapsulated in the expectation of the Messiah. Yet natural propagation of Israelite lines of descent is no guarantee as such that God will fulfill the promise to his covenant people. Fulfillment remains an act of God's free choice, as he summons whom he will to be the bearers of living hope.

Eve's first child, the first son of man, is Cain, who becomes the murderer of his brother Abel. He could not bear the fact that God looked favorably on his brother's offering, "but for Cain and his offering he had no regard" (Gen 4:5). He whom God's eyes behold stands in the light of his grace, and is "picked out" by the Lord. Yet he whom his eyes do not behold remains in darkness. That even a creature's natural existence is a matter of grace is something that emerges from the covenant that God made with Noah after the Flood (Gen 8:21). God seeks to lead his creatures to their goal despite their faithlessness, which is why he promises them that there will never be another flood to ruin the earth. This general and fundamental Noachic covenant is realized during the course of the history of Israel in a number of other covenants (Genesis 17; Exodus 19–20; 2 Samuel 7) — with the patriarchs, with the people as a whole, with the royal house. The very existence of Israel is a matter of grace, its life being thrown on God's faithfulness and mercy. It is nourished not from its own vital resources but from God's, who supports and sustains it through the terrible judgments that fall on this people.

The first patriarch of Israel is summoned by God to leave his homeland and his kin and his father's household to go to a land that God would show him (Gen 12:1-2), with the promise that he would make of him a mighty nation and bless him. Yet when this promise is to be fulfilled, and God wants to present him with a son, Abraham can only laugh. In the meantime he has become an old man. And his wife Sarah too, who had been barren all her life, is now beyond the age at which she can expect to bear a child. Thus she too can only laugh (Gen 17:17; 18:12). Yet Sarah becomes pregnant and bears a son, and Abraham calls him Isaac (meaning "he who laughs"). It is not Ishmael, born to Abraham by Sarah's maid Hagar, who will be the father of the chosen people, but the son of the free woman (cf. Gal 4:21-31). Thus at the beginning of the history of Israel there stands a miraculous birth. Sarah does not become a mother naturally but as a result of the miracle wrought in her by God.

Rebekah, Isaac's wife, is barren too, and only when God listens to Isaac's pleas does she produce twins (Gen 25:19). These children are besought from the Lord and bestowed by the Lord, and one of them is chosen and the other rejected. The mother loves the one who is chosen, and obtains for him the blessing of the firstborn by devious means, deceiving the father. Through this act — highly questionable in both human and moral terms — she fulfills the will of God, who acknowledges this son in particular: "I am with you" (Gen 28:15).

Leah and Rachel, the two sisters whom Jacob marries — Leah against his will, and Rachel after a lengthy pursuit — reflect the mystery of divine election and rejection in their jealous battle for Jacob's inheritance. At first Rachel is barren, and this is an indication that she stands out particularly in the line of grace, even though God grants sons first to Leah, whom Jacob has neglected. Rachel's son will be Joseph, thrown into the well by his brothers and sold abroad, and who precisely as a result of this becomes the savior of both Israel and Egypt. At the birth of her second son, Benjamin, Rachel dies on the way from Bethel to Ephrath (i.e., Bethlehem), and Jacob buries her in the Holy Land.

And so it is that the wives of the patriarchs of Israel experience in their own bodies the miracle of election and the misery of rejection. In the chosen people barrenness means not only renunciation of pride and joy in natural motherhood, not only failure in the eyes of the husband, but exclusion from the living promise of the people, loss of the promised land. Barrenness was a sign that God did not behold this woman favorably; and conversely, it was not the biological reality that produced the fruit — it was a miracle of the Lord. The son is not only the fulfillment of maternal longing, but the sign of divine blessing. It is in this situation that the unique distress of barrenness for the Israelite wife, and the unique joy of giving birth, is to be found. The seed that carries the living hope further is not the seed planted in the natural way: God intervenes in the begetting and bearing. Hence the sheer unbearable tension associated with procreation and birth in Israel, even though this is based primarily on the fact that it is only with the birth of a son that the wife achieves an honorable position in her husband's family, and that only a son could secure the inheritance and — as in the East in general — perform the rituals associated with veneration of the ancestors (Adolphe Lods, *Le culte des ancêtres* [Paris: Leroux, 1906]). Israel's history is — according to Wilhelm Vischer — comparable with a body filled with hope and anticipating the birth of the first son. This can be seen in the most intimate manner in the women of Israel who are asked to become mothers.

The mystery of God's election and rejection is clearly in the mind of the evangelist when he identifies four of Jesus' female progenitors as women who all mysteriously circumvent the proper line of descent (Matt 1:3, 5-6). It is in any case striking that women should appear in an Israelite genealogy, but it is even more striking that they should be *these* women and not, say, the four first mothers of Israel, or other mothers of notable sons. Clearly the evangelist intends to say something quite definite by including these names. He is faced, to his astonishment, with the fact that the history leading up to the birth of the Messiah

125

is so questionable and inglorious by human standards, conspicuously lacking, both morally and biologically, any clear line of
descent. The four women become a living illustration of the fact
that the children of Abraham are children of grace (cf. Gerhard
Kittel, *Theological Dictionary of the New Testament*, 3:1).

Tamar, the first of the four to be mentioned, is a Canaanite
and the widow of Judah's firstborn son. He leaves her childless,
his brother evades the duty of the levirate marriage, and the
youngest brother is withheld from Tamar too. She finds no better
course open to her than to obtain the seed of Judah, her father-
in-law, by devious means, in order to ensure the continuation of
her husband's line. She does this by adopting the extraordinary
means of running into him dressed as a sacred prostitute. She
becomes pregnant and bears twins, who are in conflict with each
other from birth (Gen 38:27-28). Perez, who forced his way
out, is the one mentioned in Jesus' genealogy. It becomes apparent in retrospect, ringing as a promise in Judah's words, "She
is more in the right than I" [v. 26], that Tamar simply had to
perform her service as a mother.

Rahab was also a Canaanite, and thus also a "foreigner,"
and, moreover, a prostitute (Joshua 2). She took in the spies sent
by Joshua into Canaan and hid them from the king. For this,
she and all her house were protected when the Israelites invaded
the country. Rahab acted as she did in the surprising knowledge
that God was with Israel. "The Lord your God is indeed God
in heaven above and on earth below" (v. 11). This utterance of
hers is the most comprehensive declaration of faith in the God
of Israel to be found anywhere in the Old Testament. That is
why the Epistle to the Hebrews includes Rahab — the only
woman apart from Sarah — in its list of witnesses to faith (Heb
11:31).

After the death of her husband, Ruth, another "foreigner,"
a Moabitess, accompanies her mother-in-law, Naomi, to the latter's home, Judah. Naomi was also a widow, and she was concerned to ensure offspring for her son. While gleaning, Ruth

meets Boaz, a close relation among her husband's kin. At Naomi's behest, she goes to him at night, Boaz learns of her intentions, and after the legal position has been clarified, he marries her. Ruth has a son, Obed, and his son, Jesse, will be David's father (Ruth 4:22). Ruth thus faithfully accomplished the duty incumbent on her according to Israelite law, doing so like Tamar in mysterious ways, and forcing Boaz, as previously Judah had been forced, to comply with her demands to secure the "sacred seed."

Finally, the wife of Uriah, the fourth woman listed by the evangelist and who, as wife of a Hittite, was probably not an Israelite either, commits adultery with David (2 Sam 11:4). The evangelist may well be hinting at this when, instead of calling her by her name, Bathsheba, he refers to her as the wife of Uriah. She is the wife of someone whom David eliminates by force. Judgment falls: Bathsheba's son by David dies. God, however, grants them a second son, and this son is Solomon, who is named to be David's successor as king, not without powerful assistance from his mother, following the advice of the prophet Nathan. And so Bathsheba becomes David's queen, and Jesus' ancestress.

When faced with these stories, we are at a loss if we try to evaluate them as events occurring within the framework of purely human confusion and suffering. The golden thread running through them, and which alone permits us to make sense of them and to connect them to each other, is the line of descent that the evangelist has in mind and that culminates in the birth of *the* son for whose sake these Israelite mothers were forced to struggle in such a dire fashion to become mothers in the first place. They are tools in God's hand, signs indicating that God's people is created and sustained not through natural propagation, but only through his gracious hand. Whether a mother is truly "mother of the living hope" is not a question decided through biological motherhood alone.

The question is raised and answered in a revealing way in the story of the so-called judgment of Solomon (1 Kgs 3:16-28).

127

Two prostitutes who have given birth in the same house during the same night appear before the judgment seat of Solomon. One of the two women has accidently smothered her baby in her sleep, and in the darkness exchanged the dead child for the other mother's live one. Each of the two women maintains that the baby left alive is hers. The king then commands a sword to be brought so that the baby can be cut into two halves and each of the women can receive her share. At this point the baby's real mother cries out that it should be given to the other woman rather than be killed. "Give her the living boy; certainly do not kill him!" And Solomon decides that this woman is the child's mother. Two mothers, that is, two nations, diverge in the one nation of Israel: one has a living hope, the other a dead one. The question of who is the true mother permeates the whole history of this people. Does the mother really love the child for its own sake or does she covertly love it, for her own sake, that is, as her property? Does she stand by a hope that transcends her, reaching out into a future that is no longer hers, yet for whose sake she herself lives? Here one touches on the secret of divine election. Hence we find a passage like the following: "Sing, O barren one who did not bear; burst into song and shout, you who have not been in labor! For the children of the desolate woman will be more than the children of her that is married, says the Lord" (Isa 54:1). There can be, then, a form of motherhood that transcends biological motherhood. There can be prophetic women who become spiritual mothers.

One such "mother" in Israel is Deborah, who, as judge and prophet, summoned the twelve tribes of Israel to fight a war of liberation after they had suffered for twenty years under the repression of the Canaanite kings (Judges 4). Similarly one could mention a woman like Zipporah, who saves the life of her husband Moses by circumcising her son with a flint, and touching her husband's loins [NRSV "feet"] with the foreskin in order to remind the Lord, who sought to kill Moses, of his promise, and to tie him down to his covenant with Israel through the sign

128

of the covenant (Exod 4:24-26). Or again, one could mention the clever and beautiful Abigail, who, in contrast to her foolish husband, helps David and his followers when they are on the run, and becomes his second wife (1 Samuel 25); or Huldah the prophetess, who, in the time of decline after the Exile, once again delivers the word of the Lord with full authority to his people and their king, Josiah (2 Kgs 22:14-15).

In shocking contrast to these women are those who harbor only a dead hope and therefore serve death: for example, Michal, the daughter of Saul and David's first wife, who despises David when he dances before the ark of the covenant, and is punished with barrenness (2 Sam 6:16-17); or Jezebel, the wife of King Ahab, who does wrong and whose death comes in fulfillment of Elijah's prophecy: "The dogs shall eat Jezebel within the bounds of Jezreel" (1 Kgs 21:23; 2 Kgs 9:39-40); or again Athaliah, a queen in Judah, who sought to destroy the seed of the house of David and was then slain with the sword (2 Kings 11).

All of the women mentioned, whose number could easily be increased considerably, illuminate, whether positively or negatively, what it means to be the mother of all living. The fifth woman mentioned in Jesus' genealogy (Matthew 1) is Mary. She is destined to be the mother of *the* living and thus fulfill the hope and longing of the Old Testament mothers that were directed towards the son who would be his people's Messiah.

In the New Testament the figure of the mother retreats into the background, and her task in salvation history is ended; viewed from this perspective, the question posed in the first Christian churches concerning the extent to which the begetting and bearing of children was still allowed or required, following the birth of Jesus Christ, is a justified one. Behind their asceticism there may lie a recognition that the "end time" has dawned, and what counts is to be "anxious about the affairs of the Lord, how to please the Lord," not to care about "the affairs of the world" (1 Cor 7:32-33). "Yet she [woman] will be saved through childbearing" (1 Tim 2:15), provided "they continue in faith and love and holiness, with modesty." For as long as it may please God to preserve this world and its people, children may be begotten and born as a sign of his patience, and mothers may rejoice in them as an assurance that God blesses them in their action if they are imbued with living hope. Biological motherhood as such is not something that is justified in its own right in the New Testament either, even though one may be consoled by justification if it is occasioned by the birth of *the* son. That he will grow new limbs is the promise under which every newborn baby is born, which is why baptism becomes a person's real and genuine birth. That it pleased God to become man in a woman's womb, that Mary can rightly be called "Mother of God," is the glory of the promise resting over every human mother, and at the same time is an unambiguous warning never to glorify biological processes as such.

Who was Mary? We learn only that she was a virgin from Nazareth, betrothed to a carpenter called Joseph from the house of David, a rather undistinguished descendant of the former royal lineage. We are not told anything about Mary's ancestral line. Nor is it of any importance, because in Jewish eyes it was not the biological link that guaranteed a son's rights but legal acknowledgment of him as a son by the father (cf. H. Strack and P. Billerbeck, *Kommentar zum Neuen Testament,* 6 vols. [Munich: Beck, 1922-61], 1:35).

To this undistinguished virgin, Mary, God sends his angel Gabriel. Mary is frightened when she hears his greeting: "Greetings, favored one" [Luke 1:28], just as, shortly before, the priest in the temple, Zechariah, was frightened when the angel of the Lord appeared to him. Mary is faced with a completely unexpected and unknown event, and she too, like Zechariah, is told, "Do not be afraid." The appearance of an angel signifies that an invisible realm unknown to humanity is being disclosed — heaven opens up and comes to earth in the form of a heavenly messenger. Yet where his messenger is, there is God also. Humans may and should be terrified at such an encounter. For something is happening that transcends their powers of imagination and their capacity to grasp. The angel's message of "joy" and "delight" is something completely new and unexpected breaking into human existence. In contrast to Zechariah, Mary does not doubt the angel's words; nevertheless, she frames a question based on her presuppositions about the known world and its laws: "How can this be, since I am a virgin?" Mary lacks the biological conditions of motherhood, for she has received no seed, she is a virgin. Then the angel proclaims to her the miracle of the Holy Spirit, and she accepts his word and complies: "Here am I, the servant of the Lord; let it be with me according to your word" (Luke 1:38). "Here is the whole *mysterium christianismi,* the word, and faith. The virgin could not comprehend that it could be possible for her to conceive a child. That is why the angel says to her: 'Abandon understanding. It has to be replaced by incomprehension, and you will not know how it will happen.' To which she responds: 'Let it be with me according to your word.' Therefore no one should be master of himself, but should restrain reason in respect of those matters affecting godliness and salvation and faith" (Luther, Weimarer Ausgabe, 9:625). Mary allows herself to be summoned out of her world, she treads the path laid out for her by God, she commits herself to the miracle of his grace, she trusts his promise: in a word, she has faith. "Here Mary has no example in any creature on earth that she can cling to and draw strength from; indeed, they are all contrary to her faith, for she is there all alone, about to give birth and become a mother without the intervention of a man, contrary to all human reason, sense, and conception. Do you not think that such an influx of faith will have touched her deeply? For she was flesh and blood as we are. That is why she had to let go of everything, including herself, and cling only to the word that the angel proclaimed from God" (Luther, Weimarer Ausgabe, 17/II:399).

In Elizabeth, a relation of Mary, she is given a companion, a sister, who, like her, can experience in her own body the fulfillment of the angel's promise. She was old and barren, but God miraculously granted her a son, and this son is to be the herald who goes before the Lord and proclaims his coming: John the Baptist. When Mary enters Elizabeth's house, John leaps in his mother's womb and Elizabeth greets Mary with the words: "Blessed are you among women." She recognizes her as the "mother of my Lord" and declares her blessed for having believed (Luke 1:42). Mary then sings a song of praise (vv. 46-55). It is a song of praise by someone from Israel, as sung centuries before by Hannah in the temple when God granted her a son (1 Samuel 2), and as sung even earlier by Miriam (Exod 15:20) after God had led his people through the Red Sea and destroyed the Egyptians. But there is more than this here. In Mary and Elizabeth we see what the Lord promised coming true: "Where two or three are gathered in my name, I am there among them" [Matt 18:20]. Because he is there, they bear witness to his presence by praying and giving thanks. At this point there appears for the first time the church of the new covenant.

From a human standpoint, Mary's position is impossible. According to Jewish law her betrothed should repudiate her, or even bring her to court; in fact, he wants to be lenient and have the marriage contract set aside quietly (Matt 1:19). Then the angel of the Lord appears to him and commands him to take Mary as his wife, "for the child conceived in her is from the Holy Spirit" (v. 20). Luther argues that this happened "in order that our Lord's mission should not have its origins in rumor. For if the virgin had declared publicly that she was bearing a child by the Holy Spirit, and not by Joseph, she would have had to face death. For unless she could prove it, nobody would have believed her. . . . Hence Joseph conceals the fact, so that no one sees that the Holy Spirit is at work as a pure servant of virgins. Therefore the virgin gained protection from marriage, and the Holy Spirit was able to work secretly and act before anyone could understand" (Weimarer Ausgabe, 9:629). Joseph obeys the angel, marries Mary, and acknowledges Jesus as his son, thereby introducing him into the house of David. So defenseless and vulnerable is the entry of the eternal son into this world that a simple craftsman has to help in order for his simplest conditions of existence to be met.

It was granted to Mary to be the first to experience the incarnation of the Son of God in her own body. That is the greatest mark of distinction that could come woman's way. Even if history should ascribe the historical event to a man, the story of Jesus Christ is not a story of men. Men are conspicuous by their absence at the birth of the Lord. Mary is a *virgin* mother. The great miracle of the incarnation of the eternal Son is accompanied by the sign of this miraculous birth. How much more profitable it could have been for Christian ethics if God had chosen the marriage of Joseph and Mary to be this sign. Yet God chooses a virgin, thereby excluding man's creative act. Not because virginity as such is more akin to the miracle of grace, but because it can attest that humans can approach this miracle of grace only in the role of recipient. Here God acts alone — there is no question of human achievement. Karl Barth suggests (*CD*, I/2, p. 212) that we might see in the sign of the virgin birth a sign intended as a contrast to the words of judgment in Genesis (3:16), "And he shall be your lord." When *the* Lord appears, man's lordship is disregarded. Rather, woman is accorded preeminence in a manner that surpasses every other form of preeminence.

Yet this "preeminence" is a matter of grace and not any human desert. It is the "poor handmaiden" whose lowliness God has regarded. Graced as she is, Mary remains dependent on grace. In truth, even from a Protestant point of view, she is not simply a piece of earth, a "lump of clay" (Scheeben, *Handbuch der katholischen Dogmatik*, 4 vols. [reprint, Freiburg im Breisgau: Herder, 1933], 3:456), but a human being whom God has summoned to perform the most wondrous service that a human being has ever been chosen to do. She is to be "mother of God," earthly mother of the heavenly Lord. When the early church

133

bestowed on Mary the title "Mother of God," *Theotokos,* this was because of the Son. People wanted to affirm that Jesus Christ is truly God and truly man (Council of Ephesus, AD 431). Mary's hymn of praise — the Magnificat — is a hymn by a human being from Israel to whom it has been granted to experience the fulfillment of the promises made by God to her forefathers, and who now rejoices that God has taken care of Israel. Mary stands on the threshold between the old covenant and the new. Moreover, it had to be the mother to whom it was first revealed that the son would burst the traditional barriers and that the long-awaited Messiah would be the savior of the world.

We find her, after the Lord's resurrection and ascension, in the company of his disciples (Acts 1:14). During the course of his ministry, however, according to the few places in the Gospels that mention Mary, Jesus appears to have prevented her from exercising any maternal claims on him (cf. John 2 and Luke 11:27-28). " 'Who is my mother, and who are my brothers?' And pointing to his disciples, he said, 'Here are my mother and my brothers! For whoever does the will of my Father in heaven is my brother and sister and mother' " (Matt 12:48-50). Mary becomes just one among the company of those who hear his word and follow him. She has carried out her special form of service. The dying Jesus on the cross commits her to the care of his disciple John: "Woman, here is your son" and " 'Here is your mother.' And from that hour the disciple took her into his own home" (John 19:26-27). Surely the words of the departing Lord should be taken to mean that the legitimate path for his church drawn from among Israel, and of which Mary is the important representative, leads to his disciples, that is, to the apostles, who are to be his representatives on earth. There is no other future for Mary than this. Conversely, though, since she is the church drawn from among Israel, she is the mother of the apostle, his origin, that which belongs to him. Thus the Lord has brought them together, and thus shall they remain together. The service that Mary performed is, in its uniqueness, a definitely circumscribed form of service. Her path leads into the church of the new covenant. Whoever claims more than this deviates from the gospel.

The Roman Catholic doctrine of the Virgin Mary does claim more. "The reason why Christ and the apostles did not themselves emphasize and celebrate Mary's glory is more than fully explained by the fact that the whole attention of the faithful was focused on Christ himself" (Scheeben, *Handbuch*, p. 458). "Mary conceived and bore her son regardless of her virginity, and remained virgin even after his birth," declared the church as early as the seventh century. If Mary is the Mother of *God*, it is incompatible with this unique honor for her virginity to be anything other than a permanent, everlasting one, and therefore one that is still preserved after she has given birth. *Virgo et semper virgo* is a eulogy for Mary found already in the discourse and liturgies of the early church. Mary is characterized, however, not only by lasting physical purity but also by the will to preserve this purity to the glory of God. With her question to the angel she not only admitted her actual virginity but also made a vow of eternal dedication to God. She is therefore also characterized by virginity of attitude, for which virginity of disposition is necessary, that is, freedom from all sensual impulses and desires. Thus Mary fulfills to the utmost degree of perfection the Christian idea of virginity, being *the* virgin prophesied by Isaiah (7:14)!

Mary is not only *the* virgin, however — she is the *gracious* virgin. In the unique honor of her role as Mother of God, it was necessary that she remain wholly untarnished and therefore free from original sin.

"Through a unique exercise of grace, Mary was preserved, from the very first moment of the conception, from any stain of original sin" (see B. Bartmann, *Lehrbuch der Dogmatik*, 2 vols. [Freiburg im Breisgau: Herder, 1920-21], 1:439). This was the third dogma to be developed concerning Mary, following the celebration as early as the seventh century of the feast of the Immaculate Conception (first in honor of her mother Anna, but

135

THE QUESTION OF WOMAN

soon after in honor of Mary). The church's teaching office initially exercised some restraint in respect of both the feast and the doctrinal development. Gradually, however, the "Immaculata" became a "sententia communior," or indeed "communissima." And so, on 8 December 1854, in the bull *Ineffabilis Deus,* Pius IX pronounced the dogma. A further judgment inevitably followed this, albeit one that has still not received official formulation[1] but has nevertheless long been acknowledged as the "devout opinion" of the Roman Catholic Church: "By virtue of a divine privilege of grace, Mary was, throughout her life, free of personal sin" (see Bartmann, *Lehrbuch,* 1:435). If the honor of her role as Mother of God called for a sinless beginning to her life, then it no less called for a sinless course for her life. Mary is the "worthy vessel without spot or stain." She is the Immaculate.

Sinlessness implies liberation from the bondage of death. We lack any reliable reports of Mary's death. Theologians, however, describe it as an "unforced passing away caused by her overwhelming longing and love for her son and for God," and the liturgy describes it as a "falling asleep" (see ibid., p. 444). Her sinless body, however, could not fall victim to decay, and so the "Assumption of Mary" is a "devout opinion" long since accepted by the church, and finding expression from the sixth century onward in a feast day, and has long since become part of the Catholic literature. (In this connection cf. A. von Speyr, *Handmaid of the Lord,* trans. E. A. Nelson [San Francisco: Ignatius, 1985], a book that is also instructive in respect of the literary uses of Mariology.) In the September 1948 issue of the *Schweizer Rundschau,* in an article entitled "Einem neuen Dogma entgegen" ("Toward a New Dogma"), we read that the dogma of the Assumption of Mary is ripe for formal endorsement, given that Pope Pius expressed his inclination to support it two years

---

1. This doctrine was actually promulgated a few months after this book was published. — Ed.

previously. "Unless we have been quite misled by the evidence, therefore, a formal dogmatization is imminent." A clearly developed justification for this teaching was contained in the petition sent to the Holy Father two years ago from the Faculty of Theology in Fribourg. Typically, the first reason advanced in support is this: "It was necessary that the Redeemer should be raised from the dead, and therefore too his coredemptrix. . . . It is inconceivable that the liturgical ritual practiced since the seventh century could have been mistaken" (as quoted in the *Kirchenblatt für die reformierte Schweiz*, 6.I.49, p. 10. In this connection cf. too Hugo Rahner in *Orientierung*, 31.I.49, p. 15).

And so Mary is "full of grace," as the Vulgate translates the angel's greeting (Luke 1:28). The abundance of her grace exceeds that of the angels and saints; it is comparable with that of Christ, albeit only as the light of the dawn in relation to the sun. For Mary remains a *creature*, and therefore everything that the Son possesses by his nature is hers only on the basis of grace. Yet on the basis of the unique abundance of grace bestowed on her, she is called not just to be the Mother of God on earth but also to participate in Christ's work.

Here, though, let us end with Luther:

> But the masters who so depict and portray the blessed Virgin that there is found in her nothing to be despised, but only great and lofty things — what are they doing but contrasting us with her instead of her with God? Thus they make us timid and afraid and hide the Virgin's comfortable picture, as the images are covered over in Lent. For they deprive us of her example, from which we might take comfort; they make an exception of her and set her above all examples. But she should be, and herself gladly would be, the foremost example of the grace of God, to incite all the world to trust in this grace and to love and praise it, so that through her the hearts of all men should be filled with such knowledge of God that they might

137

confidently say: "O Blessed Virgin, Mother of God, what great comfort God has shown us in you, by so graciously regarding your unworthiness and low estate. This encourages us to believe that henceforth He will not despise us poor and lowly ones, but graciously regard us also, according to your example."

> (*Luther's Works*, vol. 21: *The Sermon on the Mount [Sermons], and The Magnificat*, trans. A. T. W. Steinhaeuser, ed. Jaroslav Pelikan [St. Louis, Mo.: Concordia, 1956], p. 323)

As a consequence of our now forsaking God's will and command, we are forsaken by God and we have devoted ourselves to trivial things, and we turn the further and the more from the Creator to the creature, and we have even made creatures into a God and Creator. See now, what words these are that we offer to the Holy Virgin Mary in the Salve Regina. Who will account for it that she should be our Life, our Consolation, our Sweetness, when she is satisfied with being a frail vessel? The prayer is sung throughout the whole wide world and the great bells peal it out. It is also no better with Regina Coeli, that she is called Queen of Heaven. Isn't that an insult to Christ that one offers to a creature what belongs to God alone? Therefore let us cease from using such disgraceful words. I would be happy that she prays for me, but that she should be my consolation, and my life — I won't stand for that, and your prayer is for me equally dear as hers. Why? Since if you believe that Christ lives just as well in you and in her, then you can help me just as well as she can.

> (Weimarer Ausgabe, 10/III:321-22: Sermon v.d. Geburt Mariae, 1522)

# EXCURSUS: MARY IN CURRENT MARIOLOGICAL DEBATE

The discussion among "Mariologists," that is, Roman Catholic theologians who deal with the doctrine of Mary, revolves nowadays around the question of what share of her cooperation *(cooperatio)* in the redemptive work of Christ is to be attributed to Mary.

There is no disagreement among the Mariologists about *whether* there was such cooperation, but there is indeed disagreement about *the extent* of this cooperation. Catholic doctrine distinguishes between the objective order of the work of salvation, that is, the life, passion, and death of Jesus Christ, in other words the work with which he made amends to the Father for the offense done to him by the sin of humanity, and calls that the "addition," the *acquisitio,* to the Treasury of Grace. To this objective order there corresponds a subjective order of the work of redemption, the dispensing and appropriation of the additional grace, the *dispensatio.*

Now the claim that Mary had an active share in this subjective order through a comprehensive and uniquely effective power of intercession is something about which the Mariologists agree, whereas they part company with each other over the question of whether in addition some degree of influence of a physical kind is to be ascribed to her.

139

There is also agreement, in respect of Mary's share in the objective order of the work of redemption, and so in bringing about salvation, that she did participate in so far as she voluntarily accepted and fulfilled the office of Mother of God, thus bearing for fallen humanity their savior, and in so far as, over and above that, she gave away his body and blood in the sacrifice of the cross. Throughout all her life and suffering she was bound to him in a unique and most intimate way, and gained a store of merit on behalf of humanity.

Mariologists disagree, however, on the question of whether it is permissible to infer from this closest of connections with Christ that Mary had a direct share in the objective work of redemption of the Son: and of whether, therefore, she should be described not simply as cooperator but actually as co-redeemer (coredemptrix), and hence also as mediator (mediatrix), of all grace. A dogma defining Mary's share in the work of redemption has still to be formulated. Consequently, there is plenty of scope for theological disagreement, and the various opinions on the matter that are current at present seem to be irreconcilable.

Those Mariologists who believe that her cooperation extended as far as a direct share of her son's objective work of redemption, and that she should therefore be described as coredeemer (coredemptrix), base their view on her unique bond with Christ. Mary is not merely the earthly mother, the living "soil" from which the new Adam appeared, but she is, over and above this, his helper and the bride of Christ. As the temple of the Holy Spirit, her body bears the eternal Logos that takes upon itself her flesh, and fuses with her in the most intimate manner. This *principium consortii* is the main component of the thesis of Mary as coredeemer. Because of this unique bond to Christ, Mary has a unique calling and capability to support him in his work. Hence her place in the divine plan of salvation is quite singular. She becomes co-cause, "second principle" (Scheeben, *Handbuch*), of redemption. The theological root of this inter-

140

pretation of Mary's role in salvation history is to be found in Gen 3:15, which speaks of Mary's victory too, and Jesus' words in John 19:26-27: Mary beneath the cross.

The most important evidence from church tradition, however, is the parallel drawn from as early as the patristic period between Mary and Eve. Nevertheless, whereas the fathers — Justin, Irenaeus, Tertullian — draw this parallel only in connection with Mary's obedient acceptance and fulfillment of the role of Mother of God, modern Mariologists (such as Scheeben, J. Lebon, F. Schüth, C. Dillenschneider, J. Bittremieux, C. Friethoff, B. B. Merkelbach, etc.) interpret it speculatively to mean that *both* sexes participated in redemption as they had in the Fall. As Eve was given to Adam as a helper, so too was Mary to the new Adam, Christ. The parallel of motherhood does not exhaust Mary's significance for salvation. "God ensured that Christ was joined by Mary as co-cause *(coprincipe)* of life just as in the order of the Fall Adam, as cause of the Fall, was joined by Eve as co-cause of death." Mary's role is similar to, and blends in with, that of Christ, so that the effect produced depends directly on one single complete cause formed jointly by Christ the Redeemer and the Virgin Mary as coredeemer, by Christ the Mediator and the Virgin Mary as comediator (J. Lebon, *L'apostolicité de la doctrine de la médiation mariale* [1930]). This notion of "joint causality" is followed to its logical conclusion. Mary is "co-cause of salvation" uniquely and above all through her activity as Mother of God, in consequence of which she brought into the world its Redeemer. In faithful obedience she drew down the Son of God into her womb and prepared a place worthy to receive the Redeemer. Thus in the truest and most proper sense of the term, she paved the way to salvation.

In addition, though, she participates in bringing about salvation through her collaboration in Christ's redemptive sacrifice. This is not simply a matter of Mary's involvement through her personal merits, sufferings, and prayers, but she is literally the one who makes the sacrificial offering, comparable to Abraham sacrificing his son. Mary is not herself a priest, but she is the priest's assistant. She offers her son, her own flesh and blood, as a sacrifice.

But if Mary has helped win all salvation's graces through this collaboration in the redemptive sacrifice on behalf of the whole of humanity, it follows that one may, and indeed should, say that she took receipt of the whole merit of the redemptive sacrifice and all salvation's graces for the whole of humanity. "Just as God granted humanity its Redeemer through and in Mary, by causing his Son to become man in her womb, so too has the Redeemer bestowed his redemptive merit on humanity only through Mary" (Scheeben, *Handbuch*, p. 613). Christ poured all his redemptive blood into the heart of his mother (from whom he had received it in the first place) as she stood beneath the cross, in order to pour it through this heart, as through a conduit, over humanity at large. Thus Mary becomes the Mother of the Redeemed. After the Redeemer's death, however, Mary is united with the apostles in prayer and begs for the Holy Spirit to descend. As recipient of the life-giving power of Christ's passion, Mary was to — and in her heart was able to, as the "germ cell" of the church — prepare humanity to receive the Holy Spirit. The final form of her collaboration with the Redeemer, however, and one which is to last until the perfecting of all the redeemed is complete, consists of her most comprehensive and most effective power of intercession as Queen of Heaven, seated at the right hand of Christ.

In all stages of her collaboration with Christ, then, she is at work as active and effective mediator of salvation, through whose hand all salvation's graces reach human beings. It is through her intercession that prayers are heard, and therefore intentionally to exclude this intercession of Mary's would endanger their being heard. In conceiving and giving birth to Christ she mediated the gift of the very source of grace; through her collaboration in the redemptive sacrifice she helped win all salvation's graces; she became guardian of the whole merit of

142

redemption for humanity; she is thus the true spiritual mother of all the redeemed and the ideal model for that church without which no one receives grace at all. It can be no cause for astonishment, therefore, if the church's liturgy refers to Mary as *the* ladder and *the* gateway to heaven and *the* hope of the children of Eve.

This teaching about Mary's direct participation in the redemptive work of Jesus Christ has encountered powerful opposition from among the ranks of the Mariologists. Most prominent among the opponents are B. Bartmann, Werner Goossens, L. Billot, M. de la Taille, J. Ude, B. A. Luychex, and M. J. Congar. Others who have strong reservations are B. Poschmann and Fr. Diekamp, and two people who finally decided to reject the teaching after years of investigation are G. D. Smith and K. Lennerz. (These references are taken from Werner Goossen's book, *De cooperatione immediata matris Redemptoris ad Redemptionem objectivam*, 1939.) These Mariologists do not deny the unique bond between Jesus Christ and his mother, but refuse to draw these conclusions from it. They point to 1 Tim 2:5: "There is also *one* mediator between God and humankind, Christ Jesus, himself human." "Mary is in no respect a co-cause of salvation, for then there would be a shared act of redemption: Jesus-Mary, a combined salvation. Our faith teaches the opposite. There is only *one* Redeemer, *one* Mediator, *one* Savior. On Golgotha all graces were won through Christ, not through Mary too. This teaching stands in contradiction with Catholic dogma," says B. A. Luychex (*Onze ennheid in Christus* [1936], 2:72-73).

They make the further point that Mary too was redeemed by Christ and therefore could not have participated in his objective work of salvation. "The Virgin was in need of redemption, herself. . . . Thus her situation in no way differs from ours in this respect. . . . If then, by this title of coredeemer that some modern authors have not hesitated to give her, we understand some contribution on her part to the very price of redemption paid by Jesus Christ, this could be put down to those pious excesses, which may be excused for their good intentions, but which nonetheless, speaking objectively, are in direct opposition to the most fixed dogmas of Catholic teaching" (L. Billot, *Marie mère de grace* [Paris: 1921]).

Similarly Bartmann, in *Christus ein Gegner des Marienkultes?* (Freiburg: Herder, 1911), opposes the notion of Mary's participation in the objective work of salvation: "Mary . . . is not a mediator in the objective sense, as though she had taken an active share in Christ's work of salvation to the point of completing it, so that we ended up with two people to honor as Redeemer, one of them a female coredeemer (coredemptrix)."

The charge of contradiction is directed too at the claim that Mary, through her merits, won for us all graces. "There can be no question of Mary mediating grace on account of her merits. For immediately the possibility of merit via Mary already presupposes redemption through Christ, who alone has already won all graces for the whole world. . . . The reason why we have earned . . . all graces from the outset is Christ alone, according to his humanity, offering everlasting satisfaction to God through his passion and his death. Only Christ could offer the satisfaction required. And since he alone has already earned all graces for the whole of humanity, one can no longer say that Mary earned graces for humanity through her merits" (J. Ude, *Ist Maria die Mittlerin aller Gnaden?* [Bressanone: 1928], p. 17).

These Mariologists, though, want to see Mary's participation in the redemptive sacrifice limited to the *moral union* of the Mother of God with her son, reflected in the way she accompanied him and suffered with him in the most intimate manner. But it is impossible to talk of a sacrifice or sacrificial offering in the direct sense because Mary had absolutely no power of control over her son. He offered himself up in obedience to the Father. He paid the purchase price and brought about our salvation in reconciliation. Mary had *no* part in this ransom. "Et in quonam sensu, salva iudicio Ecclesiae, censemus negandum Matrem Redemptoris immediatae cooperatum esse ad effectus redemptionis

144

objectivae seu, ut aiunt, ad acquisitionem gratiarum [And thus we are of the view, subject to the judgment of the church, that we should deny that the Mother of the Redeemer had a direct share in effecting objective redemption or, as is said, in winning graces]" (Goossens, *Cooperatione,* p. 158).

We find, then, that thesis and antithesis stand in stark opposition to each other. Goossens observes quite rightly that there is no reason for being allowed to proceed more simply in respect of the issues relating to Mary than in respect of other items of dogma. Piety, he continues, has never been harmed by the need to present a solid case, and there is no question of being fearful for the honor of the Virgin, since a solid theological justification, far from casting a shadow over the truth, is the very thing to bring it to the light of day (ibid., p. 28).

Two years ago there was published in Germany a book by the Roman Catholic theologian Dr. Heinrich Maria Koster, *Die Magd des Herrn* (Lahnverlag, Luneberg a. d. L., 1947), which attempts to reconcile thesis and antithesis in a synthesis. The author expresses the hope that he will be able to present new perspectives "based on revelation and the philosophy of St. Thomas Aquinas." He skillfully applies "the kernel of Thomistic metaphysical method," namely, the "magnificent and profound concept of act and potency," to Mariology. From revelation, however, he latches on to the covenant, where God and humans are no longer isolated from each other, but commit themselves to a shared existence within a reciprocal relationship. "The religious relationship collapses . . . if humans drop out just as much as if God does" (p. 96). "What occurs between God and humans in the religious act is actually the highest example of what the doctrine of being can articulate in association with the two related notions of act and potency" (p. 101). The eternal Word as the actual part, and human beings as the potential part, represent the two poles that support the religious act, the covenant. Since Christ occupies a place in the covenant that is uniquely his, that is, he stands as a person on God's side — he is after all not a human but a divine person; he only assumed human nature — what emerges in the salvation event when the eternal Word encounters humanity in its need of redemption is that the corresponding place, where a human person sets up what is human against the eternal Word, is left unoccupied. The figure of Mary seems made to fit into precisely this gap (p. 126), Christ the divine person, Mary the human: an "immense personal space" is thus created for Mary. She constitutes the very pinnacle of human personhood, and in this sense it is possible to identify not Christ but Mary as humanity's high point (p. 133). This is not to take anything away from the undiminished humanity of Christ. It is merely to place Mary in this "free space," where everything can be maintained in respect of her that ever was maintained by proponents of the coredemptrix thesis. Now, though, "all subtleties, tortuous twists and turns, and artificialities" associated with this thesis "disappear." "The picture loses all its traits of being contrived and artificially constructed, gaining instead the liberating appearance of something that has evolved naturally" (p. 322). Conversely, however, all the objections raised by opponents of the thesis — or at least all those that could be regarded as incontestable on the basis of official Catholic dogma — become irrelevant, because there is simply no possibility of blurring the distinction between the Redeemer and the Mother of the Redeemer. For if the coredemptrix thesis propounded hitherto was concerned to attribute to Mary all the redemptive functions of Christ, only in a somewhat watered-down form, the synthesis now being proposed starts from the assumption that a "contrasting double element" is required for the "complete realization of redemption": God *and* humanity! Mary represents, as both matter and recipient, humanity in need of grace. "In this way she is by the same token coredemptrix and co-cause of redemption, just as matter along with form is the crowning principle of being" (p. 325).

Indeed, all difficulties are now resolved. But the price of their resolution is surely the complete sacrifice of *theological*

146

thinking in favor of *philosophical* thinking. Surely the magic formula that opens all doors here is the Aristotelian-Thomist system of the polarity of act and potency, of form and matter. And surely the attempt, which is indeed "tortuous" and "artificial," to deck Mary out with the merits of grace after the fashion of Jesus, thereby elevating her to the position of equal partner and collaborator, arises from a theological inhibition against applying the principle of polarity to the action of God in Jesus Christ in this uninhibited way. One may legitimately query whether this "inhibition," which admittedly seeks to avoid dualism, but still wants to safeguard Mary's participation in bringing about salvation, is not at bottom a much cleverer and therefore much more dangerous attempt to elevate pardoned humanity, in possession of and with the authority of this grace, to the status of a "second cause," thus resorting here too, with the assistance of philosophical concepts, to theological speculation. In any event, these two avenues of thought, the coredemptrix thesis and Koster's "synthesis," do not appear to be fundamentally irreconcilable.

But those representing the opposing view, the antithesis, will not be able to accept this "synthesis." It is true that the "blurred boundary" between Christ and Mary as found in the coredemptrix thesis has now been avoided, but at the cost of dividing the redemptive work of Jesus Christ into two mutually dependent halves. The person and work of Christ are incorporated into a metaphysical system that has as good as nothing to do with the scriptural basis on which these Mariologists are seeking to defend *one* Redeemer and *one* Mediator.

Reviewing this summary of the "Mariological debate," which has only sought to indicate briefly what the main arguments are, we Protestants will have no great difficulty in reaching a conclusion. It is obvious that we support the antithesis. Yet even here we have to ask: Can the appeal to *one* Redeemer, and *one* Mediator, retain a powerful and credible ring if there is in principle recognition of a *cooperatio* on the part of us created

147

humans, if the notion of *Christ alone* is in effect changed to the notion of Christ *and* the pardoned creature, Christ *and* Mary, God *and* humans? Are not those Mariologists consistent who follow through from the notion of cooperation to that of coredemption, from *cooperatio* to *coredemptio*? Must not the opposition of the others suffer from the fact that they want to call a halt at a place where there is no longer any halt because the prior warning signals were ignored? And can an appeal to Holy Scripture retain any compelling force within a mode of theological thinking that recognizes alongside both Scripture and the equally important concept of tradition that of the teaching office of the church? which, in other words, has given up the notion of *sola scriptura*?

"Subject to the judgment of the church" was how these theologians qualified their opposition. Church practice and the church's liturgy have long since overtaken them, and it seems only sensible to assume that, when it comes, the dogma that will be formulated will lay out Mary's share in the objective work of redemption to a maximum extent. It will then emerge that this does not after all mean a shaking of the foundations for those Mariologists who are currently opposed to this. Catholic thinking is never exclusive in character, and the face that the Roman Catholic Church presents to the world is never unambiguous. We are faced with a grandiose "both . . . and . . ." held in balance by a relationship between God and humanity that is to be thought of as indeed damaged by sin but not destroyed, and in which, therefore, the pardoned human being, in addition to having the "one consolation in life and in death," must still reach out for another.

# ❖ 5 ❖

# CRITICAL VIEWS

Gertrud von Le Fort has shown very impressively, in her book *Die Ewige Frau* (The Eternal Woman) (Munich: Koesel & Pustet, 1934; reprint, Olten: Otto Walter AG, 1947), how Roman Catholic Mariology has influenced Catholic teaching about women and Catholic analysis of what it means to be human. She is concerned to bring out the symbolic nature of the position of women. "Symbols are signs and pictures in which ultimate metaphysical realities and destinies are not perceived abstractly but brought home by means of analogy or parable" (p. 5). The symbol itself remains unaffected by its empirical realization, and retains its validity even where it is neither seen nor denied. Like every truth about women, it is possible to infer from the image of the Eternal Woman an understanding of the symbolic meaning of the feminine. According to the author, what she is referring to is revelation through woman; what is revealed, the object of revelation in itself in its metaphysical being, is not something that can ever be usurped by woman, because revelation of any being always has, on earth, a double character, a male and a female: Mary, as representative of all creation, represents man and woman alike (p. 7). The epithet "eternal" used of her does not, therefore, refer to "eternal" traits of the image of women as they actually are, but to the cosmic-metaphysical face of woman, the feminine as mystery, as the original and also the final image in God (p. 12).

The most powerful utterance that has been made in this respect about woman is to be found in Catholic dogmatics, where a woman has been declared "Queen of Heaven," and this one woman, the "blessed among women," is, even if she is infinitely more than this, the figure embodying the symbol of the feminine. In her the metaphysical secret of woman has become open and visible (p. 14).

Even if the Marian doctrine was late in being promulgated, it nevertheless stands at the beginning of the mystery in terms of its content — indeed, at the ultimate beginning; for the *Immaculata* signifies the proclamation of what a human being was like as a created being that had not yet fallen: the unspoiled face of this created being, the image of God in a human being. This is what the Virgin represents. On her humble *fiat*, given by way of answer to the angel, depends the secret of the salvation of humanity. Humans have nothing to contribute to their salvation but a readiness for unconditional devotion. The doctrine of Mary is, in a nutshell, the doctrine of humans' cooperation in their own salvation (pp. 15, 25). Mary is therefore not only the object of religious worship but "the religious" medium itself through which God is worshiped. She is the "power of devotion" of the cosmos in the form of a betrothed woman. Her temporal-human image is inaccessible, resting as though veiled in the mystery of God. The "veil" is the symbol of the metaphysical on earth and thus the symbol of the feminine, for the feminine has a special affinity for the religious. The astonishing achievements of woman are tied to the religious sphere; they occur beneath the veil, in devotion. On the one hand, where there is devotion, there is also a ray of the mystery of the Eternal Woman. On the other hand, where woman centers on herself, the light of the metaphysical mystery goes out: by emphasizing her own image, she destroys the eternal image. The Fall is therefore at its most profound the fall of woman. Creation fell in her feminine substantiality, for it fell in its religious aspect (p. 20).

Woman in time appears to constitute a full half of all human

150

being and happening, and hence of history. In fact, however, man and his work supply the content of historical life. He dominates the great political events of the world, he determines the rise and fall of spiritual cultures; indeed, even religion is shaped by man in its historical forms and primarily represented by him. "Wherever one listens to the spirit of the centuries, one hears his voice" (p. 33). The question arises as to whether the feminine mystery also signifies devotion in the sense of a metaphysical renunciation of historical life. Or perhaps a new criterion of historical evaluation would be appropriate.

Woman realizes her destiny in the three categories of *virgin*, of *bride* or helpmate, and of *mother*. Each of these three — *virgo*, *sponsa*, and *mater* — means fulfillment of the life of woman, each in its own way (p. 56). And in each of these three forms what counts is to reproduce the image of Eternal Woman and hence to gain the mystery of the Feminine Form.

With the dogma of the perpetual virginity of the Mother of God, the church affirms for all time the independent significance of virginity, thereby according it its own dignity. Virginity is not — as it is currently taken to be — only a condition (merely the prelude to marriage), or only a tragedy (if this condition becomes permanent), but a value. The virgin symbolizes the religious emphasis on, and affirmation of, the value of the individual. Her place is not as a link within the chain of generation — she concludes generation, facing it in solitariness, and living directly for God (p. 41). Her existence signifies renunciation and sacrifice, and hence the church's liturgy places her alongside the martyrs. The consecrated Virgin, though, utters the *fiat mihi* with reference to her unmarried state, thereby becoming the representative of her solitary sisters. God grants her fulfillment in life through the mystery of love on a higher plane than the natural one. It becomes apparent from the figure of the consecrated Virgin, Christ's *sponsa*, what the hidden meaning of every virgin is — a meaning embodied in even the most unprepossessing of them (p. 44). Corresponding to the religious significance of the virgin is her temporal significance. She, who concludes generation in order to emphasize the value of the individual, at the same time secures generation, protecting marriage and maternity by her sacrifice. If that is not widely known, it only goes to show that this too happens behind the veil concealing all feminine action. Virginity signifies strength, for man as for woman, and therefore signifies in a special sense empowerment to achieve. Woman's achievement, properly speaking, is charismatic, and thus it too occurs in the stance of the *ancilla Domini,* in the form of cooperation, in the pattern set by Mary (p. 53).

Between the figures of virgin and mother stands that of bride or of man's helpmate in every kind of varied form conceivable. In the grandiose landscape in which woman is situated according to the dogma, *virgo* and *mater,* both of which are united in Mary's title as Eternal Woman, form the two cornerstones or pinnacles between which there stretches the wide valley of immeasurable possibilities for the man/woman relationship. Even the bride is bearer of an independent secret. The church, in recognizing a childless marriage as also fully valid and indissoluble, confirms the independent dignity of being a bride, that is, not only the girlish figure of the wedding day, but also the bridelike character of the wife in relation to the husband in the miracle of ever renewed love. Mary is the eternal bride, and so the features of Eternal Woman shine forth over this way of life too.

As the consecrated Virgin, the Bride of Christ, constitutes the high point of the issue of virginity, so too the sacramentally bound consort constitutes the high point of the *sponsa* line of thinking. Behind it stands the abundance of creative possibilities between husband and wife: the nonsacramentally bound wife, the friend, the beloved, the helpmate. All of these are illumined by the light cast by the nuptial Mass. There is also a *sponsa* as bride of the masculine spirit (p. 59). The husband "recognizes" in the wife the other dimension of human being. Polarity means

152

totality, yet it represents the presupposition of every great creative achievement. That is why the husband needs the wife, but the wife "recognizes" [him] in devotion (p. 61). Just as the husband only succeeds in recognizing the wife as he approaches her in love, so too he only recognizes himself completely in her love. If the Virgin assures man of the lonely value of culture, the individual, the helpmate, assures him of the cooperation of half a world. Woman is never a real agent in her own right, but always an agent in the context of cooperation. The domineering creative characteristics of man are only one half of creative reality; the other half is humility (p. 73).

Yet what is cooperative is also cocreative. Woman as the one cooperating in concealment represents the anonymity of God as the one side of everything creative, which man can only share by stepping into line with woman (p. 74). The totality of creativity is concluded with the working together of anonymous and recognizable forces. If one of the two halves is omitted, this causes a curious wobbling in the image of the other half. Woman has no other way of making the feminine count and thus of truly being the one half (p. 89), of remembering the primal powers and primal role of the feminine. The destruction of the equal balance and hence of the totality of being can occur both through the hubris of the self-proclaiming man and also through the woman renouncing her symbolic character by denial or surrender. It is not the man but the woman who must save the threatened image, for it is only through her that the reflection of the feminine can once again become visible in the face of the man. The hour of God's help is always also, as the religious hour of humans, the hour of woman, the hour of the creature's cooperation in the work of the Creator (p. 95). For God's creative power can only come down from heaven to renew this earth if from earth it is met by the religious power, the readiness of the *fiat mihi*. Thus woman is appointed guardian of the religious sphere.

The figure of the mother, finally, is that of the timeless woman, the same in all epochs and peoples. In the form of a

153

virgin, woman faces time alone; the *sponsa* shares time with her husband; the mother overcomes it. The maternal woman is the greater conqueror of everyday existence, and all the more so when her victory is least noticed. As a mother, woman signifies not simply one half of reality, as does the *sponsa*, but "her share is probably much greater than a half" (p. 116). As a ray of the maternal happiness and maternal dignity of the eternal mother falls on every mother, so too a ray from the "mother of compassion" falls on her. "To descend to mothers" means descending further than to the physical mother; it means to seek *the* Mother in the mother herself. It is not physical motherhood alone that creates motherliness. It can happen that the strong desire for a child turns out to be a very feminine form of egoism, an illusion or delusion of genuine motherhood. King Solomon, however, did not allow himself to be deceived by this illusion, seeing in his wisdom that the one mother's readiness to give up the child was proof of her being the genuine mother!

Just as woman as childbearer extends life into infinity, thus overcoming time, so too as carer and protector she contributes an infinite moment to time (p. 128). That is why the church sees in physical motherhood the original and primary destiny of woman, perceiving in her the mother of the people and of all peoples. She grants the child earthly life and by the same token the precondition of redemption. Yet nature is here too but a prelude to grace. The second and higher birth is baptism, and so the church becomes the true womb, and the natural mother takes second place to the supernatural one. If the character of nature as the prelude to grace becomes apparent in the *physical* mother as such, then in the *Christian* mother this character is recognizable as the cooperation of creation with divine action. Thus the great theme of the Marian dogma can be heard here too: the cooperating creature is the daughter of Eternal Woman, the reflection-like bearer of the *fiat mihi*. Alongside the bearer of religious fatherhood, the spiritually procreative priesthood of the man, there stands within the church the religious mission of woman, her apostolate as motherly mission. The church could not entrust woman with priesthood, for then the church would have destroyed the real significance of woman in the church, would have destroyed part of the church's own being, which woman was entrusted to represent symbolically. Woman is called above all to represent the hidden life of Christ in the church, and therefore her apostolate is primarily an apostolate of silence. Here in the religious sphere the mother becomes really the all-embracing form of woman's life (p. 151).

The Christian woman exists in the great divinely ordained orders of *virgo, sponsa, mater,* each of which signifies a complete form of fulfillment, but also a link to the shared primal image (p. 153). In each of them what counts in the first instance is the unfolding of this image, this picture, in order to depict it in part, but at the same time what counts is to reassemble the whole picture: the virgin must pick up the thought of spiritual motherhood, but the mother must return again and again to spiritual virginity. The salvation of each woman is indissolubly linked to the picture of Mary and to Mary's mission. The conscious composition of the "Eternal Image" is only possible for individual women in the stance of *ancilla Domini,* of constant readiness to be at God's disposal. "Mary alone signifies, not simply the salvation *of* woman, but also salvation *through* woman" (p. 154). If what matters for the individual woman is the recovery of the "Eternal Image," what counts for the world is the restoration of its power. The actual salvation of the world depends on the example set by Mary becoming visible even in regard to man. The proclamation to Mary is, at its most profound, the proclamation to the whole of creation. The *sponsa* that represents the *virgo* and the *mater* before man's eyes represents the Marylike qualities of man's life and work, and portrays it as half of his reality. Woman's mission "soars beyond woman" and touches the secret of the *world:* Eternal Woman represents the whole of creation. The restoration of the "Eternal Image" through the Marian mission of woman culminates "in the representative role of the representative of creation — Mary stands for her daughters, but her daughters stand for her." Again and again "the proclamation to Mary *precedes* fulfillment through Christ, concealment *precedes* appearance, the humility of readiness *precedes* redemption, the Yes of creation *precedes* the arrival from on high" (p. 157).

What does all this add up to? The salvation of the world is tied up with the restoration of the image of Eternal Woman by women, and its revitalization for the world. Mary is a symbol that has taken on a definitive shape, that is, a figure representing eternal truth about humanity. She is the inviolate face of creation, the image of God. And because she is a woman, women as the daughters of Mary stand in a special relationship to the religious realm, being appointed its guardians. They may and should follow the course laid down by Mary in one of the great Christian roles of *virgo, sponsa,* and *mater,* so that the reflection of the Eternal Image may reappear in the face of man too. Man's historical achievement remains uncontested, but is of only relative significance in this framework. For even the figure of the *sponsa,* which functions as the practical complement of man, and also represents to him the figures of the *virgo* and the *mater,* is in fact encompassed and exalted by the latter two, which are themselves really Marian figures. Only the priest as the spiritually procreative father still has access to these. Mary has completely fulfilled what a creature can hope to do on the basis of grace: she is *the* coworker, *the* cosavior. She is so in her unconditioned readiness for devotion. In her, devotion as the secret of redemption is visible in a unique manner, superior to any that is found in any other creature. People are therefore to take their direction from her, being summoned by her to imitate her.

This means, however, that humans are confronted not with a reality but with a symbol that has taken on a specific shape, in other words, with a . . . myth. They lose themselves in the boundlessness of their own existence. They remain in conversation with themselves, and therefore lonely. The Mary of Catholic

156

Mariology, the "Queen of Heaven," is not the virgin from Nazareth of whom the evangelist tells; she is the bold dream of the exaltation and glorification of creatures endowed with grace. This dream, however, misses out on the reality of encounter with God's living, free grace. Grace is trapped in the "Eternal Image."

The New Testament knows of an "image of God" too, meaning "his beloved son" (Col 1:13, 15; cf. 2 Cor 4:4; Heb 1:3; also Rom 8:29; 2 Cor 3:18). The true God exists by being father, by containing a legitimate counterpart for himself within himself. He does not exist in solitariness, but in this duality. God does not need his creatures in order to avoid being solitary. The very possibility and actuality of his creating a world rests only on the fact of his existing with his son as his counterpart, on the fact that God is love. This Son, however, the person whom he loves and who loves him in turn, is Jesus Christ. He is the firstborn of all creatures, for he was in the beginning with God. In him God created all that is, in him the eternal Word became flesh, and the divine name became a human one. Thus he reveals the being and the will of God, and in him God pours out his heart (Luther). Yet if God has set up his image in the middle of his cosmos in this one person, then in him there has been passed a verdict on humanity itself. To be human now means: to be a fellow human being of this one person. We cannot repeat his existence, and neither can we imitate it. Jesus Christ is *the* image of God, exclusively. What happened in him happened once and for all. The difference between this person and all other people is not a quantitative one, but a fundamental and therefore insurmountable one. For only he is God and a human being in one person, only he is therefore the person who exists wholly for God and also wholly for human beings. His life, the life of Jesus the human being, is devotion.

Yet since it is the life of Jesus the human being, he is not only someone who is wholly dissimilar to us, but our human brother, born of a woman, someone who shared the conditions of human existence, and hence is someone who is also similar to

157

us. To be confronted with Jesus is to be confronted with God and with our fellow humans also. The true human being, who is precisely the one for whom Jesus exists, is not solitary; he is by nature a fellow human being. Therefore an anthropology based on Christology cannot take seriously the notion of an isolated human being. This person is a fiction. The Word of God that comes to us in the life of Jesus the human being summons us to recognize and comprehend our humanity on the basis of his life. The secret of our existence is disclosed in the light of encounter with him. If we have him as our fellow human being, then the very nature of being a fellow human becomes intelligible to us as involving being someone who belongs to our own existence. Then we recognize that the gracious love of God that we meet in Jesus was at work already at our creation. "Male and female he created them." We do not lack a human being attached to us in the most intimate and original figure. And therefore we should not *want* to be without this companion. For the Thou and the I are not by nature strangers to each other; they are implicated in each other's lives. Only together are man and woman the human being for whom Jesus lives, and hence the true human being. Humanity is not an ideal and not a virtue; humanity is the fact of human beings having been created in this inherent relatedness, in this duality. This is not something that can be resolved into a higher unity; it is an unalterable condition of being human. There is no *humanum* above man and woman. And precisely the fact that there is not, constitutes grace.

The reality of Jesus the human being discloses to us our human reality and causes us to recognize the offer to us that it contains and that we may gratefully accept, in the readiness now truly to be those who we are. For only thus, only in this gratitude of recognition, will man and woman live in genuine solidarity and hence in genuine partnership, where neither woman triumphs ultimately over man, nor man over woman. Jesus Christ is the head of the body, namely, of the church (Col 1:18). Because he bound himself to us to such an extent, by living and dying for us, that he no longer lives alone, no longer lives without us, and for just this reason is the image of God, we may resemble him, may therefore imitate him in respect of also not living without our fellow humans. His life for and with us offers us release, and frees us of all self-redemption, yet points us unmistakably toward our brother (Matt 25:40). That is where he wants to be sought and found. Our "devotion" can be at best a faint token of our gratitude for his devotion, which was not more complete than ours, but was of a fundamentally different nature. He "did not regard equality with God as something to be exploited" [Phil 2:6], that is, he gave up his divine glory for our sakes, he came to us, became human like us. In him there comes to us God's love in human form. In his unceasing love for us he treads the path from the heights to the depths in order to seek and to find us *there* as the people we are: sinful, fallen humans who would never have been able to find their way to him on the strength of their own resources. *This* human being is the honor and dignity of the human race. We, however, may recognize in his light what it means to be human. He does not lead us into unrest, he makes no demands for wonderful achievements, he turns us completely into people who have been showered with gifts and who can only burst forth in jubilation like Mary: "The Lord has looked with favor on the *lowliness* of his servant" [Luke 1:48].

This, then, is the difference between "Marian" and "christological" anthropology. People who take their direction from the "Eternal Image" remain profoundly solitary, however powerful the stimuli to *imitatio* may be that come from this image. They follow their ideal. And that is why fellow humans necessarily become exponents of this imitation, of this impressive achievement, why the complementarity of man and woman becomes the complementarity of "masculine" and "feminine" as the two halves of being that must necessarily be kept in balance if their totality is not to be put at risk. Women, however, surpass this complementarity in their special disposition to the religious realm, in those Marian figures of virgin, bride, and mother. Yet if the Eternal Woman is a myth, then people who get their bearings from it necessarily pass by reality. The actual encounter of man and woman is an episode in the career of the daughter of Mary.

A recent book attempts for the first time to deal with the question of woman on the basis of existentialist philosophy. It is "Facts and Myths," the first part of Simone de Beauvoir's work *The Second Sex.*[1] This book constitutes a decisive attack on the sort of treatment of the question of woman that has been customary up to now, and is especially instructive in its confrontation with the Catholic understanding of this issue. Simone de Beauvoir takes as her starting point the fact that woman finds herself in a world determined by men where she is only *l'Autre,* the other, and hence the object of the male subject. How can woman fulfill herself as a human being in this condition? How can she win her independence and thus come of age when she is closeted in this degree of dependence? The issue here is not that of woman's "happiness," but of her freedom (p. 29). It would be pointless raising the issue if woman were burdened by an unalterable physiological, psychological, or sociological fate. According to de Beauvoir, however, none of these factors, not even the physiological ones, are *existential* factors that govern the here and now. In other words they are not factors that are necessary to a person's being in the world, in the way that, say, death is, or human corporeality. The particular structure of a person's body, including its sexual differentiation, forms part of that person's particular situation and is therefore not unalterable. It is in principle possible to imagine a human society that reproduces itself by parthenogenesis (p. 36). Certainly, biological factors — such as menstruation, pregnancy, birth, menopause — are ex-

1. Page references have been changed to give the corresponding passage in the ET by H. M. Parshley (reprint, London: Picador Classics Edition, 1988). — Ed.

tremely weighty conditions of the female situation, but they are not sufficient to justify a hierarchy of the sexes or to condemn woman to play a subordinate role throughout her life (p. 65). Only by concentrating on the *human being* is it possible to draw a distinction within the human species between male and female. The human being, however, is not a being that is simply there, but constantly makes itself what it is; it is not a piece of nature, but an idea becoming history. Hence woman can be compared with man only in her *becoming*, in her *possibilities*, not in the fixed form of what she was yesterday and is today.

In contemplating a being that is transcendent and transitional, one can never close the files. The biological features of woman need to be understood in connection with their ontological, economic, sociological, and psychological context, all of which need to be fully appreciated, if they are to be correctly understood and evaluated. The contributions of psychoanalysis and historical materialism should, despite occasional insights, be rejected, because neither Freud's sexual monism nor the economic monism of Engels takes into account the totality of human existence. Psychoanalysis regards woman's social aspirations merely as an expression of her sexual inferiority complex, while conversely Marxism seeks to explain her sexuality merely in terms of her economic situation. In seeking to understand woman, one should surely not despise certain contributions from biology, psychology, and historical materialism; however, the body, sexual life, and the technical sociological conditions only exist for people in any concrete sense when they are grasped in the context of a summary overview of their lives. The value of muscle power, of the phallus, of tools can be grasped only within a world of values; yet that world is conditioned by the basic project in which existents develop their individual projects in the direction of being.

In the second part the historical conditions for woman are shown on a wide canvas: in a world that has always belonged to man, and has done so for hitherto inexplicable reasons, since the reasons offered up to now do not appear to hold water. Admittedly, in the light of the insight furnished by philosophical existentialism, it is possible to understand how the hierarchy of the sexes could not come about. Whenever two human categories appear, each seeks to assert its dominance over the other; if both persevere in this attempt, there arises, whether in hostility, whether in friendship, in any case in tension, a relationship of reciprocity; yet if one of them is preferred, it triumphs over the other and takes pains to maintain it in subjection. It can readily be understood that man has the will to rule over woman. But what advantage empowered him to be able to assert his will? It was man who conquered the world. He sensed his power, he set himself goals, he worked out ways for realizing those goals: he realized them as an existent. By contrast, woman, in giving birth and suckling, exercises only natural functions, and fails to carry out any real deeds!

Here lies the key to the secret. At the level of biology the species is preserved by creating itself anew, but this creation is only a repetition of the same life under different forms. It is only when the human individual transcends life through existence that values are created and pure repetition is denied. It is not by giving life, but by risking their lives, that humans rise above the level of animals: that is why, among humans, dominance goes not to the sex that bears children but to the one that kills. In behaving dominantly, man encounters woman: for she too is an existent, and her project too is not repetition but striding forward into a different future. Deep down in her being she finds confirmation of masculine claims. Her misfortune lies in the fact that she is biologically destined to repeat life, after seeing with her own eyes that life does not contain within itself the justification of its own being: this justification that is, after all, more important than life itself. She sees and acknowledges the values that have been realized in practice by man. He opens up the future into which she too strides. Women have never actually contrasted feminine values with masculine ones. This division has been

162

invented by men. They created the feminine realm in order to confine women within it.

Yet beyond all sexual differentiation the existent seeks his justification in the movement of self-transcendence: even the subordination of woman shows that. What women demand today is to be recognized as existents in the same way as men, and that existence should not be subordinated to life, or the human to the animal. The feminine is more closely tied to the species than is the masculine. Through the invention of tools, life for man has become activity and project, whereas motherhood makes woman a prisoner of her body, like an animal. Man does not want to be repetitive over time; he wants to be master of the moment and to forge the future. Masculine activity, by creating values, has elevated existence itself to a value, and thus raised it above life's confused powers; at the same time it has forced both nature and woman into subjection.

De Beauvoir shows how man's domination of women has worked out over the centuries, and comes to the conclusion that there is still no true equality of the sexes even today. We are in a period of transition. The world, which has belonged to men for so long, is still in their hands. Women do not want to be elevated in their *woman*-ness, but want transcendence to triumph over immanence in them as in humanity in general; they want to be given both their abstract rights and their concrete opportunities, without which freedom is a form of mystification. This desire on their part is in the course of being realized. The situation is not yet stable, however, and therefore it is very difficult for women to adjust. They find that factories, offices, universities are being opened up to them, yet marriage continues to be regarded as one of the most honorable careers for them, freeing them from all other forms of participation in social life. As in primitive cultures, the sexual act is for them a form of service for which they have the right to be paid more or less directly. Because of this state of affairs, a woman needs to make much more of an effort morally than does a man to choose the path of independence. It has not been sufficiently widely understood that even temptation is an obstacle, indeed, one of the most dangerous (p. 169): the economic advantages that the man has, his social value, the advantage of marriage, the usefulness of a masculine support — all of this obliges women to seek to please men. They remain, all things considered, in a position of dependency. It follows that woman does not so much recognize herself and choose herself to live as an independent existent but rather as someone determined by man.

In a third part, de Beauvoir expounds man's impression of woman as expressed in mythology and literature. Just as it was economically advantageous for men to keep women in a position of dependency, so too it served their ontological and moral pretensions. People remain solitary when confronted only by nature, whether touching a stone or eating a fruit. For there is only another presence where there is a self-consciousness different from my own. Therefore only the existence of another person can pull people out of their loneliness; only this other existence allows them truly to fulfill their being, that is, to fulfill themselves as transcendence, as a project (p. 171). Yet this alien center of freedom, while confirming my freedom, also conflicts with it. Each consciousness raises claims to being the only one to act as subject. Each one attempts to fulfill itself by enslaving the other. Conversely, the one enslaved experiences itself as central, and sees the other to be only peripheral. This tragedy can be overcome by the free recognition of each by the other, in which each simultaneously and reciprocally posits both itself and the other as object and as subject. However, the friendship and generosity that this recognition of these freedoms fulfills in concrete terms are not virtues easily achieved; they are surely the highest form of human fulfillment; here the individual stands in truth. Yet this truth is one of continuous struggle. It requires one to surpass oneself constantly. In other words one can also say that the individual human being achieves an authentic moral stance upon giving up "being" in order instead to exist. In this "conversion," one also gives up all possessing, for to possess is a way of getting hold of being. Yet this conversion, in which true wisdom wins, is never something that is completed; it always demands to be done again, it demands constant exertion. Life thus becomes a daunting risk whose outcome is never assured. Yet man does not like difficulty and is afraid of danger. He dreams of peace in the middle of discord, and of an opaque abundance that he is nevertheless conscious of.

This dream takes on the shape of woman. She is the longed-for mediator between nature which is alien to him, and what is the same as him. She does not confront him with the hostile silence of nature, nor with the hard demand for mutual acknowl-edgment. In a unique way she is self-conscious, yet it seems possible to possess her in the flesh. Thanks to her, therefore, there is a way of escaping the inexorable dialectic of master and slave. Woman accepted this domination by man, and he did not feel — as with slaves — threatened by the possibility of being turned into an object by the other. Thus woman appears as the peripheral that never becomes central, as the absolute other, without reciprocity.

All creation myths give away the secret of this conviction that is so priceless to man, including the Genesis myth, which, thanks to Christianity, has come to prevail in Western culture. Woman is not created at the same time as man, and she is taken from another substance — the rib of the first man. Her birth was not independent. God did not create her for her own sake, he destined her for man. He gave her to Adam to rescue him from his loneliness, and she has both her source and her goal in him; she supplements him in respect of what is peripheral and ines-sential (p. 173). Thus she appears to be a privileged item of booty. She is nature elevated to consciousness and she is a by nature subordinate consciousness. Thus man's wondrous hope appears to be fulfilled: he can complete himself as a being by carnally possessing another being, and can have his freedom confirmed through a free person being submissive to him. No

165

man wants to be a woman, but every man wants women to exist. His presence in the world is an independent fact and a right, while that of woman is just a sheer accident, an *accidens*, though a very fortunate one (p. 173).

Thus man seeks in woman the other both as nature and as something akin to himself. She is not the only incarnation of the other; there were times when other idols replaced her: thus, for example, the cult of the Führer excluded every other kind of cult. Every myth presupposes a subject whose hopes and fears are projected onto a transcendent heaven. Women, who did not posit themselves as subjects, have not evolved any myths; they dream through the medium of men's dreams. Men have invented figures in whom they glorify themselves: Hercules, Prometheus, Parsifal. A myth is not readily grasped, and the myths that men have invented about women are unusually complex and elusive: Delilah and Judith, Aspasia and Lucretia, Pandora and Athene, or even Eve and the Virgin Mary — in each case focused on one figure. She is goddess and maiden, she is the source of life and she is the power of darkness, she is the elementary silence of truth and she is the lie, she is the warrior and the wet nurse; she is man's precious possession and his downfall; she is everything that he is not and that he would like to have, his negation and his raison d'être (p. 175). In the figure of the "Great Mother," whom he has dethroned, she encounters him at her most elusive and most sinister. Not until the advent of Christianity was he able to take control of her.

Paradoxically, Christianity proclaims the equality of man and woman. It spurns the flesh. If woman renounces the flesh, she becomes equal to man, saved, like him, by the Redeemer. The divine Redeemer is male. Humanity, however, must cooperate in its own salvation. It is summoned in its humblest and most unnatural form. Christ is God, but it is a woman, the Virgin Mother, who reigns over human creation (p. 203). Mary's virginity is the negation of the flesh. While denying Mary the character of wife, one elevates her as mother. However, she is

166

only elevated as she accepts the subordinate role allotted to her. She is the "servant of the Lord." For the first time in human history the mother kneels before the son, voluntarily acknowledges her inferiority. In the cult of Mary we see the ultimate and highest victory of man: the rehabilitation of woman through the completion of her defeat. Now he has escaped forever: the earth takes hold only of his bones. The fate of his soul, however, is decided in realms where a mother's power counts for nothing.

Through her subjection woman can acquire a new role in man's myth: she is honored as a vassal. As a servant she receives the greatest divinization. She becomes a spiritual mother, protector of the poor and suffering, with humanity hidden under the folds of her cloak. The Christian God has all the sternness of justice; the Virgin has all the sweetness of compassion (p. 213). Everything now gets transposed: black magic becomes white (p. 204).

Thus man projects onto woman all his desires and fears, and in doing so he bypasses the reality of woman. Through religion, tradition, language, poetry, the cinema, the myth of woman penetrates the facts of existence, and lived experience and independent judgment become displaced by an idol. In a final section de Beauvoir shows vividly, through various samples taken from literature (Montherland, D. H. Lawrence, Claudel, Breton, Stendhal), how here too the mythological image of woman is at work.

In the eyes of man, the "true woman," *la vraie femme,* is to a considerable extent woman affirming herself as the "other." Today a contradiction exists in man's attitude: on the one hand he accepts and promotes the fact of the equality of woman much more than previously; on the other hand he wishes that she would remain peripheral. Woman, however, cannot reconcile these two conditions, vacillating between one and the other, and losing her balance in the process. For man there is no hiatus, no break, between public life and private life. The more he is in action, the more manly he appears. The humane values and the values of vigor and vitality are united in him. For woman, by contrast, they conflict in her image of man, and also in herself, insofar as she has not freed herself from this image. It seems as if something new is seeking to establish itself these days — a new aesthetic understanding and also a new erotic understanding. Perhaps they will be accompanied by new myths! In any event it is very difficult for women today to reconcile their conditions as independent individuals with their lot as females. And this is the source of so many illnesses and complaints for women. It is undoubtedly more comfortable to put up with blind slavery than to work for one's liberation. A retreat is not possible. The only thing one can do is hope that men, for their part, will accept the situation that develops. Only then can women live through it without inner conflict. Only then, when she no longer has to sigh beneath the chains he puts on her, when she has liberated herself, only then will she be a human being in the fullest sense.

The question being posed here relentlessly is the question of women's liberation, and it is directed both to men, who have to a considerable extent prevented this liberation, and continue to do so, and also to women, who have complied with men's wishes, and to a considerable extent continue to do so, because it seems more advantageous to comply than to revolt in a world that is economically and ideologically determined by men.

By her own admissions de Beauvoir seeks to apply "existentialist morality." According to existentialist thought (of a Sartrean kind), people are "thrown into the world, into nothingness," in order to choose themselves and persist through all facticity. A person "is" not, but "becomes," and becomes, moreover, what he or she chooses to become. People are the totality of their actions. Thus existence precedes essence: it creates its own essence in autonomous freedom. People fulfill their freedom only by ceaselessly transcending themselves in the direction of new freedoms. And there is no further justification of their present existence than this march onward into an infinitely open future. Each time that transcendence slips back into immanence, however, existence is degraded to an "in itself" *(en soi),* freedom into facticity. This "fall" *(chute)* is to be regarded as a moral error if it is something desired by the subject, and as repression if it is inflicted from outside. In both cases it is absolutely evil. That is why all individuals who want to justify their existence have an indescribable need to transcend themselves. Woman as subject shares this need, and it is her tragedy that, through the fault of man and through her own weakness, both together, she is again and again forced to live as object.

Holy Scripture also knows that human beings "become" through repeated acts of decision making. One does not find there either any general images or programs. When, within Christianity, such notions nevertheless occur, and one finds reference being made to "Christian woman," "Christian family," or even "the Christian West," these are sociological rather than biblical notions. People hear God's summons cutting straight through all facts and conditions, and they respond to this call with their existence. "Go from your country and your kindred and your father's house to the land that I will show you . . ." — that is the command delivered to Israel's patriarch [Gen 12:1]. And he makes ready and goes. The Bible too thinks historically. It does not proclaim an idea of God; it bears witness to the history of God's dealings with humanity.

In purely formal terms, then, there are some similarities between biblical and existentialist thought. Hence it is possible that Christians and existentialists can meet in their judgment and perspective on a specific issue. In my opinion, then, the analyses of the situation of women that de Beauvoir proposes are broadly correct and therefore instructive for us too. For even when she recklessly exposes numerous issues she is carried along by the honest effort to reveal suffering in its full extent, in order, by doing so, to help to overcome it. Why should we not be able to go some of the way together?

However, we should not allow ourselves to be deceived; our points of departure and our goals differ. De Beauvoir explains in her introduction to the second volume, "Woman's Life Today" (to which unfortunately we cannot devote detailed attention here), that it is not her intention to proclaim "eternal truths" but merely to indicate the common basis on which each individual female existence has to be shaped. In fact, though, in the first pages of her first volume she makes an observation of a very fundamental kind: that the sexual differentiation between people does not belong essentially to their existence in the world, as do, say, death or corporeality. The structure of the body is a given that human beings have to handle freely. The division of individuals into male and female is not an ultimate condition. "The fact that we are human beings is infinitely more important than all the peculiarities that distinguish human beings from one another" (p. 737).[2]

In comparison, the biblical witness recognizes in the fact that humanity was created as man and woman the basic structure of human existence. There is no human form of being that is beyond or above man and woman. Humanity exists only in the dissimilar duality of man and woman. Sexual differentiation, which in any case is the only kind of differentiation among humans in contrast to all other creatures, is thus the primary condition of human existence. That humanity "is" in no other way, that it "becomes" in this encounter in which it finds itself, was a conclusion we reached on the basis of Genesis 1 and 2 and Ephesians 5, recognizing the natural correspondence between this and the divine mode of being. Here the complementarity between man and woman receives its real dignity, its true equality, and its ultimate solidarity.

It follows necessarily that the [Christian] understanding of the "freedom" or "liberation" of woman has to differ from that of the existentialist, even though the latter undoubtedly has some justification as a corrective, and therefore should not be simply rejected out of hand. Man is condemned to be free if God does

2. Both volumes are bound in one in the English translation. — Ed.

not exist (J.-P. Sartre, *Existentialism and Humanism,* trans. Philip Mairet [reprint, London: Methuen, 1968], p. 34). The existentialist is not out to prove God's nonexistence: that particular issue is not the decisive one. Rather, the decisive problem is for human beings to rediscover themselves and to become convinced that nothing can liberate them except themselves. "In this sense existentialism is optimistic, it is a doctrine of action, and it is only by self-deception, by confusing their own despair with ours, that Christians can describe us as without hope" (ibid., p. 56). Humanity, then, is put here in God's place. By the same token in our opinion, humanity is burdened with a degree of responsibility that simply must occasion fear — virtually deadly fear. For how is the responsibility to be borne? Existentialists save themselves by turning optimist and thinking that, like Munchhausen, they can pull themselves out of the swamp by their own hair. De Beauvoir's contribution to the woman question must also be called optimistic in this sense despite its realism.

Whenever the Bible talks about human freedom, people are not summoned to win their freedom; they are told that they may live as "free persons" because that is what they are. They are not on the way to this goal — they are on the way from it. Anyone hearing this testimony and accepting it will certainly not become a quietist, but, in their concrete life decisions, they will practice the freedom they have been given with the same zeal that the existentialists put into exercising their freedom, as they think they must. They will throughout choose and act as free individuals right across the gamut of given facts. In the security of this freedom they do not have to chase after some "image of man," but are permitted — without fear — to know that this prison too has been broken open. Where men and women bear mutual witness to that in the reality of their existence, they stand in the genuine complementarity that no longer admits of either inauthentic domination or inauthentic subjection.

# ❖ APPENDIX ❖

## THE MINISTRY OF WOMEN IN THE
## PROCLAMATION OF THE WORD (II)

IN a report on "Women's Life and Work in the Church," which presented study materials from the churches of fifty-eight countries to the First Assembly of the World Council of Churches in Amsterdam in 1948, we find the remarkable observation that what had emerged during the course of the enquiry was that the views being gathered could be classified according to denomination. Thus the Congregationalists, the Quakers, and the Salvation Army — in other words, those churches and organizations in which the congregation is invested with all forms of ministry — were everywhere very open-minded in dealing with this question, since they "have a good conscience. They have accepted complete equality of status, and complete professional equality, for men and women." They do run into difficulties over practical issues, but "their standpoint is clear in respect of what they regard as Christ's teaching and example" (p. 7). The report notes further that it is the churches in the Anglican tradition, especially in England, that concern themselves most with the question of the position and activities of women. They do not all reach the same conclusions, "but about one thing they all agree, namely, that women cannot be ordained" (p. 8).

---

This essay arose out of a talk given on 18 January 1951 in the Basel Student Christian Union.

In the churches of the Reformation, however, which operate in the middle between these two extremes to right and left, considerable uncertainty was registered about women's participation in church work. According to the report, on the one hand "a fair degree of inflexibility" was encountered on the issue, while on the other hand, admittedly, a markedly more relaxed attitude was found, rooted probably in the Reformation understanding of the "priesthood of all believers." On the whole, however, we in the Lutheran and Reformed churches were said to be in a state of some confusion regarding the position of women in the church and especially in respect of their ministry in the proclamation of the Word. Here the question definitely becomes a theological problem: Is it possible and is it permissible for women to participate actively in the proclamation of the gospel in the church services? In Lutheran terms: Is it permissible for them to exercise the "spiritual office"? A very objective and thorough investigation of this question was carried out by a working party in Germany during the war years under the auspices of the Confessing Church. A collection of historical and exegetical material brought together as part of this investigation is available in a duplicated report [edited by Dr. Hannelies Schulte], showing how seriously leading German theologians, both male and female, have dealt with this problem.

If we leave aside the various biased arguments that are adduced in opposition to women's participation in the ministry of the proclamation of the Word, two questions remain that deserve to be taken seriously:

I. Does the New Testament contain an authoritative concept of office that by its very nature excludes participation by women?

II. Does the Pauline reference to women's position of subjection bar them from participating in the ministry of the proclamation of the Word?

# I

Under the old covenant, in Israel, there was an office to which only men could be called, namely, the priestly office. Only the priest was permitted entry to the Holy of Holies in the temple. He mediated between God and the people by presenting the sacrifice of atonement on the altar. After Jesus Christ made atonement once and for all, there can no longer be a priestly office in the sense of the old covenant. (Cf. Eduard Schweizer, *Das Leben des Herrn in der Gemeinde und ihren Diensten* [Zurich: Zwingli, 1946].) Now all members of the community have access to the Holy of Holies, now all are taught by God (1 Thess 4:9), now all have received the Spirit (Gal 6:1). Jesus Christ alone, however, is the high priest (Heb 7:26-27), and is so, moreover, in such a way that he is simultaneously the sacrifice of atonement. The New Testament no longer works with a notion of a bloodless repetition of this sacrifice of Golgotha in a sacrament on an altar — such as the Roman Catholic Mass purports to be (typically enough, there is therefore in the Catholic Church still a sacramentally consecrated priestly office open only to men!). "You are a chosen race, a royal priesthood . . ." — this is addressed to the whole church (1 Pet 2:9). Jesus Christ alone is the office bearer, who celebrates the liturgy. The term used in the Septuagint for the priestly office, *leitourgia,* is used in the New Testament exclusively with reference to Christ — with two exceptions (Rom 15:16 and Phil 2:17). The church's activities are described, however, as *diakonia,* service or ministry. All human actions can henceforth only be forms of service to the actions of the Lord himself. In secular Greek usage *diakonia* means serving at table (Luke 17:8; John 12:2; and Luke 12:37; cf. also Luke 8:1-3; 10:40; and 22:26), and thus a plain and lowly form of service. The content given to this concept in the New Testament is new. For in contrast to Greco-Roman thought, which held service in low regard and in whose eyes the master who was served was superior to the servant, a reevaluation now

175

occurs. "I am among you as one who serves" (Luke 22:27). This is said by someone who is master in his kingdom. Jesus Christ is not only officiator and celebrant, he is also servant or deacon. It follows that his disciples too are under instruction to carry out this reevaluation and reorientation that have become a reality in their Lord. "But whoever wishes to become great among you must be your servant, and whoever wishes to be first among you must be slave of all. For truly the Son of Man came not to be served but to serve, and to give his life a ransom for many" (Mark 10:43-45).

This path from above to below stands in total contrast to the natural movement of human life. It is the kingdom of God that is breaking into the world in this way, secretly. To understand this movement, or in other words, to follow the Lord along this path, necessarily implies suffering in this world. It is a matter of service to the point when one lays down one's life. And there is no escape: "Whoever serves me must follow me" [John 12:26]. Those who stand in this following are his, those called by the Lord to the living communion of the Holy Spirit. It is the *communio sanctorum*, the communion of the saints, who have received this commission to serve. This communion is "an act emanating from the innermost heart of God, in whose performance it becomes true that in the midst of their words and their work, in their actions and their suffering, something that is truly for the whole world, though not yet truly realized by the rest of the world, and that must indeed be communicated to the rest of the world by them: that Jesus Christ is Lord" (Karl Barth, *Die Schrift und die Kirche*, Theologischen Studien 22 [Zollikon-Zurich: Evangelischer Verlag, 1947], p. 25). Christians serve this Lord by simultaneously serving each other. Subjection under his lordship is realized in practice in subjection among each other. "Like good stewards of the manifold grace of God, serve one another with whatever gift each of you has received" (1 Pet 4:10). It is the gift of the ascended Lord through his Holy Spirit that enables and justifies this service. The true bearer of all gifts of grace is he, the Lord, himself. He grants the members of his body a share in these gifts (cf. Rom 12:3; 1 Cor 12:7; 11:19; Eph 4:7). Not every member receives the same gift, but each one receives his or her own individual gift, and each one, with that individual gift, is necessary to service, to ministry, in the church, and precisely "the members of the body that seem to be weaker are indispensable," says Paul (1 Cor 12:22). They all need each other; all serve to build up the body of Christ. There is no mention of any distinction of the sexes in this connection. Men and women alike, as members of the body of Christ, receive the Holy Spirit, and men and women alike, therefore, are called to service in the church. "I will pour out my Spirit upon all flesh, and your sons and your daughters shall prophesy" (Acts 2:17). They all count as one in Christ Jesus, there being neither male nor female (Gal 3:28).

One form of service, or ministry, does, however, come to occupy a special position: the ministry of the apostles. Hence it appears first in the list of the gifts of the Spirit mentioned by Paul (1 Cor 12:28; cf. Eph 4:11). Yet its being placed first by the apostle in this way is not merely about temporal sequence but is also a reference to the significance attached to the matter. For an apostle is an eyewitness of the risen Lord, appointed directly by him to his service. "What we have heard, what we have seen with our eyes, what we have looked at and touched with our hands . . ." (1 John 1:1). "Am I not an apostle? Have I not seen Jesus our Lord?" asks Paul (1 Cor 9:1). He was called through a special appearance of the risen Lord, belatedly, "as to one untimely born," and, moreover, "last of all" (15:8). With his call, according to the New Testament, there is an end to people being called directly by the risen Lord. From now on, all ministry, all service, can only be ministry or service to the word of these first witnesses, transmission of the apostolic kerygma. Through this word and through his Holy Spirit the Lord governs his church. "Whoever listens to you listens to me" (Luke 10:16).

This unique distinction and position of the person of apostle in the church and in comparison with the church finds its counterpart — and not an inconsiderable one in relation to the problem in hand — in the fact that the circle of the apostles is exclusively male, that not a single woman belongs to it. Nor may we have recourse, at this point, to the women to whom the risen Christ appeared on Easter morning. Admittedly he appears to the women first (according to Matt 28:9-10, to several, but according to John 20:14-15, only to Mary Magdalene), enjoining them to go to the brethren and tell them that they have seen the Lord. This meeting and this commission are doubtless a unique distinction proper to members of the communion from Israel who are following their Lord; it is the first of the chosen people that is being honored here. One cannot read into this any kind of appointment to an apostolic ministry. Their commission is a more limited one, both in time and in terms of content: once it has been carried out, by the same token it is at an end. The proclamation of the crucified and risen Lord will not be carried beyond the boundaries of Israel into the gentile world by these women, but by the apostles sent by the Lord and whom he prepares for this ministry by himself breathing the Holy Spirit on them directly (John 20:21-22). They will be his messengers, and bearers of the witness that calls the church into being, a witness that the church can transmit and serve.

The complementarity of apostle and church is thus not extended into a complementarity of "office" and church. The whole ministry of the church, including the ministry of communicating the gospel in word and sacrament, is subordinate to the apostolic kerygma. Indeed, Paul identifies kerygmatic gifts and ministries first — and nobody will doubt that they occupy a central position — but he does not basically set them apart from other forms of ministry (Rom 12:6-7; 1 Cor 12:28; cf. also Eph 4:11). This is not to deny that from the very beginning there were ordered and permanent ministries in the church, but only such as fitted into the whole ministry of the church. The church *as a whole* is invested with all forms of ministry and is given the authority to appoint individual members, and thereby takes responsibility for the outward mode of existence of these members. With such a vocation and such a commissioning the church can but be obedient to the call that comes from the Lord, and can thus only recognize the gifts that he has bestowed on each of his servants. This capacity to recognize gifts is itself a gift, and the act of calling members is a charismatic act of the church in prayer. With its decision it can but serve the decision of its Lord.

I should at least mention, though, that there is also one strand in the New Testament that emphasizes "offices" more strongly than do the Pauline Epistles (for what follows see Eduard Schweizer, *Die Gemeinde nach dem Neuen Testament*, Theologischen Studien 26 [Zollikon-Zurich: Evangelischer Verlag, 1949]; and "Die Urchristenheit als ökumenische Gemeinschaft," in *Evangelische Theologie* 10 [1950/51] 273). In the Jerusalem church — as in the Palestinian churches generally — Jewish patterns continued, and thus in respect of the "offices" in them these churches differed considerably from the Pauline churches. One may therefore ask whether the early church may not have had a different "concept of church" from the one apparent in 1 Corinthians 12 and 14. The question can be put even more sharply in respect of the post-Pauline churches as reflected in the Pastoral Epistles, for these had clearly become more rigid in their structures and had "established themselves in the world." The boundless uncontrollability of the charismatic gifts, as Paul knew them, now appears to have become in a particular way institutionally tamed, and it is questionable whether the gifts of grace still form the basis of ministry now or whether the "office" now guarantees the gifts of grace. For example, Timothy is admonished, "Do not neglect the gift that is in you, which was given to you through prophecy with the laying on of hands by the council of elders" (1 Tim 4:14), or "rekindle the gift of God that is within you through the laying on of my hands" (2 Tim 1:6). Here we are no longer far removed from the Roman Catholic notion of the sacramental ordination of the priest that

179

bestows on him the authority to continue the priestly office of Christ, and thus from the notion of habitual grace. Still, we must be careful and not forget that even in the Pastorals "it is not an office or an officeholder, but the church that is the 'pillar and bulwark of truth'" (1 Tim 3:15; see Schweizer, *Gemeinde*, p. 18). The authority of Timothy and Titus — for these are the two individuals to whom the letters are addressed! — is subordinate to that of the apostle. They act under his commission and conspicuously lack the authority to initiate matters, but have to "continue in what you have learned and have firmly believed" (2 Tim 3:14). It follows that their ministry forms part of the general ministry of the church, and their priority in relation to other ministers is limited to the fact that they were called and commissioned directly by the apostle. He grants them some authority, for example, that of appointing presbyters and teachers, but this delegated authority does not place them in that unique relation to the church in which the apostle stands; it empowers them as important members of the church to participate in the ministry of the Word, to which, like all other members, they are subject.

It would, then, be a distortion of both strands of thought in the New Testament if one were to try to construct a "Jewish institutional church" and contrast this with a Pauline "charismatic church of the Spirit." For Paul the victory won through the death and resurrection of Jesus Christ was the "latter end of the days" in a quite different way from that in which it was understood in the earliest church, and therefore for him the break with the past had to be achieved more radically. This does not imply that for Paul tradition was not still a living thing, or that he had no notion of well-ordered discipline in the church. He warns the church in Corinth in particular against an unduly charismatic understanding of their Christian freedom, referring them to the word of the cross and hence to the obedience proper to a church awaiting their Lord in the period between his resurrection and his return. The kingdom of God has not yet come, we still live in faith and not by sight, the building up of the church is still not complete. Nonetheless, the early church is not simply a continuation of the Jewish pattern of congregational organization. The spirit alive in it is the spirit of the new covenant, and knowledge of Jesus' fight against all assumed authority is clearly apparent in the saying handed down by Matthew: "But you are not to be called rabbi, for you have one teacher, and you are all brothers [NRSV margin]" (Matt 23:8-9). Here again, then, there is no office that is not a form of ministry or service.

The contrast between officeholder and church, or congregation, which has also become an ever more pronounced feature of the Protestant church, is alien to the New Testament, as is any distinction between "clergy" and "laity" in the church. "You . . . have received the Spirit" [Gal 6:1]. This view was also shared by those churches which, in contrast to the Pauline churches, displayed Jewish or even Catholic traits.

A "concept of office" such as is proposed by A. F. C. Vilmar can hardly be justified on the basis of the New Testament (cf. Vilmar, *Dogmatik* [Gütersloh: Bartlesmann, 1874], 2:275). He infers from article 5 of the Augsburg Confession "that for the achievement of faith a special, divinely appointed office is necessary, and faith and salvation in the church; in other words the continued existence of the church is bound up with the presence of this office, so that the church is formed and preserved through the *ministerium ecclesiasticum*. The church, therefore, has and possesses nothing and gives itself nothing from this store of blessing, but conducts itself only as recipient" — not, say, in relation to the Holy Spirit, but in relation to this "office" that is handed on from person to person, notably "through the laying on of hands which, as the transmission of the direct mandate of Christ, bestows the Holy Spirit in a totally real way." "In the spiritual office Christ is the judge of the world, and it is according to their conduct in relation to the holders of this office that one day the masses will be judged (cf. Matthew 16 and 25)" (*Dogmatik*, 2:322). According to Vilmar, however, this office — in

181

contrast to Catholic teaching — cannot be deduced from the apostolate, but rather "originated *beneath* the latter on the instruction of the apostles as a special appointment of Christ's" (*Dogmatik*, 2:274). Vilmar has produced here an interpretation of the Lutheran confessional writings that is surely not in accordance with their intent.

The Lutheran confessional writings do refer to a "spiritual office," the office of preaching, but this is conferred on the whole church. The "keys" do not belong just to certain people but to the church, and they do so directly. The church calls specific members, and it is God himself who makes this decision through human means. Recognition of the charismatic gifts of the members and thus their divine calling is itself a gift of grace, and their being called by the church is thus a charismatic act. Only in this sense can ordination also be described as a sacramental action (Apology for the Augsburg Confession, XIII, pp. 12-13). This "spiritual office" has been ordained by God for all times and peoples, and hence forms part of divine law. By contrast, the detailed interpretation of the office — for the "spiritual office" as such can never be realized except in connection with other functions — has been allocated to the decision of the church here and now, and is therefore worked out in accordance with human law. It is open to believers, in obedience to divine law, to introduce church ordinances or to change existing ones. It follows that the question of whether a woman can be called to the ministry of the proclamation of the Word, that is, to the office of preaching, cannot be given a negative answer *iure divino*, but has to be left open, and also, according to the Lutheran understanding of the office, has to be left to the decision of the church.

The Reformed concept of the office does not in principle present any difficulties for the participation of women. There is here no trace of a spiritual "office" of the kind found in the Lutheran confessional writings. Calvin, as is well known, recognized four offices: teachers, pastors, presbyters, and deacons. "The right order is imparted when all even to the least are obedient to Christ as sovereign King; when they are guided by His Spirit, and the church thus manifesting itself as His body, . . . in which each serves the other according to the gift which is given," says Calvin (Wilhelm Niesel, *The Theology of Calvin*, trans. Harold Knight [Philadelphia: Westminster, 1956], p. 200). Despite this, however, sad to relate, it is all too often precisely in Reformed circles that one comes across considerable inflexibility regarding women's participation in the church's ministry of the proclamation of the Word. (See the instructive exchange among Gertrud Herrmann, Pastor D. Wilhelm Rolfhaus, and Karl Barth that appears in the *Reformierte Kirchenzeitung* [1932], nos. 25, 28, and 30 under the headings "Ungehorsam gegen Gottes Gebot?" [Disobedience to God's Command?] and "Der Schrift gehorsam" [Obedient to Scripture].)

One may infer from the preceding remarks that no notion of an authoritarian "office" can be based on the New Testament that necessarily excludes women's participation as a matter of principle. In the New Testament, "office" means service, ministry. This is something to which all members of the body of Christ are called, each in accordance with the gift they have received. To designate *one* of these forms of ministry in terms of Old Testament priesthood can be done only if one wants to attribute to this form of ministry the authority of a mediating ministry between God and the church. Then, however, one begins to encroach on the authority of Jesus and to recognize with the Roman Catholic Church the continuation of Christ's priesthood but without being able to share the Roman Catholic understanding of the sacrament. The central significance of the ministry of the proclamation of the Word can really be fully appreciated only where it is truly a question of ministry of the Word, that is, where the Lord himself declares his support for the preacher's word, and his Holy Spirit makes it God's word. That is the miracle from which the church draws its life, and along with the church, the minister of the divine word. He has no proprietal claim on grace; it has to be constantly bestowed on him anew. Where this is recognized, the "officeholder" renounces all presumed authority and reaches out toward this gift, which is the only thing that can bestow authority on the officeholder and which renders his or her ministry, that of the proclamation of the gospel, "miraculous" too.

## II

Paul's instructions to the Corinthians (1 Cor 14:34-35) appear to constitute a veto threatening the entry of women into the ministry of the proclamation of the Word: "women should be silent in the churches. For they are not permitted to speak, but should be subordinate, as the law also says. If there is anything they desire to know, let them ask their husbands at home. For it is shameful for a woman to speak in church." Clearly Paul does not base this teaching on an authoritarian notion of office — the passage comes at the end of his remarks about gifts and the forms of ministry based on them — but on the position and function of women.

It is useful at this point to recall the specific context that evoked these words in the first place. Paul is talking about the order of worship in the Corinthian church, an unusually spiritually rich and "talented" congregation (vv. 1, 4-5), but now on the point of letting its riches become fatal by seducing its members into holding a conception of their congregation as an "enthusiastic" one. The Corinthians are in danger of misunderstanding the freedom they have won in Christ, of thinking that they are their own masters and can decide for themselves to which authority they want to submit themselves. They are "puffing themselves up" (4:6, 8; 5:2) and behaving as though everything they have were theirs by right rather than something that had been given to them. This makes it apparent, however, that with all their spiritual wealth they are thinking "still of the flesh" (3:3-4). By withdrawing from the authority of the apostle Paul,

184

and thus from the authority of the Word, they also lose the unity that only the Word can bestow. Discord and jealousy break out in their ranks. Paul reminds them that "in Christ Jesus I became your father through the gospel" (4:15). He exhorts them to be imitators of him and to submit alongside him to the word of the cross that they seem to think they can circumvent in their enthusiastic anticipation of the kingdom of God. According to Schlier, the main concern of 1 Corinthians is the relationship between gnosis and agape, knowledge and love (*Evangelische Theologie* 10 [1949] 462). And Adolf Schlatter contends that the epistle has only one theme, "to justify apostolic authority, which the church may not repudiate" (cf. *Paulus, der Bote Jesu* [Stuttgart: Calwer, 1934], p. 5). There is in fact no contradiction between these two views, but substantial agreement.

I might add, in particular reference to the passage under review, that what is highlighted in chapters 12–14 is the relationship of charisma and ministry. The tension involved in this relationship becomes particularly acute in the congregation's meetings for worship. The Corinthians' enthusiasm calls into question the aim of these meetings, namely, the edification, the building up, of the congregation — instead of using their gifts to serve this end, they want to indulge in experiences of ecstasy. There are those who speak in tongues even when nobody interprets their meaning. There are prophets who prophesy even when their voices are drowned out by other prophets so that their words cannot be heard by the congregation at large, and it is not the case that "all may learn and all be encouraged" (14:31). Certainly we have here gifts of the Holy Spirit, but clearly even they can be used in inappropriate ways, not as part of genuine ministering, but in effusive self-indulgence. "Let all things be done for building up" (v. 26). If this aim is lost sight of, if the spirits of the prophets are no longer subject to the prophets, then clearly all is confusion. "God is a God not of disorder but of peace" (v. 33). The church will be built up only through the knowledge that is rooted in love, and therefore only through the charisma that, instead of being self-serving, is put into the service of the Lord and his church.

Paul knows that in the church women too — like men — receive the gifts of the Holy Spirit, including kerygmatic gifts. In 1 Cor 11:5 he gives some instructions for the behavior of women who minister in the proclamation of the Word: A woman should not prophesy and pray with her head uncovered, but should be sure to cover it as a way of bearing witness that even during her ministering she is aware that she is carrying it out as a woman and hence has no thought of denying her position as a woman even there. We are not at present concerned with the much debated contradiction between 14:34 and 11:5-6 [see above, pp. 98-102], but with the fact that in both passages what interests Paul most is that during a church service a woman should be conscious of her responsibility as a woman. Clearly this aspect of her ministry strikes the apostle as being of essential significance for the edification of the church.

We see, then, that the difference in the position of men and women in the church, that is, in the place where two or three are gathered together in the name of the Lord and he is in their midst, is of considerable relevance — it is not resolved in some kind of equality that obliterates this difference. Nor is this the meaning of Paul's words in Gal 3:28: the unity in Jesus Christ, in which "there is no longer male or female; for all of you are one," does not mean that individuals cease to be what they are, but that despite this they are all absorbed equally into this unity as children of God. And particularly as children of God they will acknowledge the special responsibility required of them as men and as women. And it is the responsibility of women that is of particular interest to the apostle in the context of the church's order of worship. In 1 Cor 11:3 he specifies the order in which men and women are placed in relation to each other with the words "the man is the head of the woman" [NRSV margin]. The person designated "head" within a particular order takes the leading role, takes precedence over any other partner or partners. In the case in hand, the other partner is the woman. And when Paul exhorts women "to be subject," he is exhorting them to recognize and acknowledge this position that has been accorded to them. That is what "annoys" us. Does he, then, as a man of his time, see women as inferior creatures who must comply with the leadership role of men? This is the inescapable conclusion if one takes this passage in isolation rather than in the context of Pauline thinking overall. A woman's position is in no way inferior to a man's for Paul. This is apparent from the fact that he places the sentence "the man is the head of the woman" in a parenthetical passage, which, admittedly, has caused exegetes much shaking of heads as they have read and interpreted these words.

Thus Hans Lietzmann, for example (in *An die Korinther I.II*, Handbuch zum Neuen Testament [Tübingen: Mohr, 1931], p. 53), observes that "the main line of argument in the following verses (vv. 3ff.) is not fully comprehensible. . . . What we do not understand is why Paul did not omit v. 3 together with the forced play on words in vv. 4-5, and in both cases appeal instead quite straightforwardly to what was the prevalent custom." Similarly Wilhelm Bousset notes (in *Schriften des Neuen Testaments,* 3rd ed. [Göttingen: Vandenhoeck & Ruprecht, 1917], p. 128): "The reason why the apostle makes this remark (which incidentally subordinates women to men in a manner foreign, for example, to his own more liberal opinion in Gal 3:28) is not at all clear," and he goes on to ask whether perhaps verse 3 might not be "a later marginal annotation."

What Paul has in fact done is to insert the anthropological saying about men and women between two utterances about Christ that cast light on the position of men and of women alike. "Christ is the head of every man" (v. 3a), he begins, and then concludes, "God is the head of Christ" (v. 3c). Christ himself, then, exists both in a position of superiority and in one of subordination; indeed, he is *the* superior and *the* subordinate, he is *the* Lord and *the* servant, as crucified *and risen* he is king of his kingdom, and as risen *and crucified* he is subservient to his Father's will. Contrary to a widely held view, therefore, Paul is not intending at all to establish a "hierarchy" (God — Christ — men — women) according to which men would have direct access to Christ but women's access would be mediated via men. What he intends, rather, is to highlight the independent and direct relationship of each and every person in *their* place and *their* position. The positions of men and women alike have been sanctified by the fact that both of them were designated by Jesus Christ, and that Christ's promise and command rest over both of them. In the light of this equality any judgmental comparison of the respective positions of men and women becomes irrelevant, and each person can only recognize and acknowledge in creaturely gratitude their own particular position as the one granted to them by God as the proper framework of their existence. "As other things are not within human power, neither is it in human power to determine whether someone is to be a man or a woman. The sun cannot say: I want to be the moon, and the moon cannot turn itself into the sun; each thing and person has to remain as created by God" (Luther, *Predigten über das 1. Buch Mose,* Weimarer Ausgabe, 24:52).

The fact of my being a man or a woman is part of the uniqueness of my existence that has been determined by the will of the Creator. His command requires me to acknowledge this will even with respect to my gender. That it lays this particular claim on me, irrespective of whatever else it may say, and that men and women in their individual masculinity and femininity are affected by it, each in their own place, accounts for the independent responsibility of both in their mutual complementarity. That the man is the "head," that he leads and the woman follows, that he calls and the woman responds, can only be taken to mean that he is summoned *first* to watch over the order in which they have been placed together. He in particular is constantly tempted to misuse the power, the *exousia,* entrusted to him, in their mutual relationship. He certainly should not "rule

188

over" woman. As is well known, the words "and he shall rule over you" (Gen 3:16), often quoted in this connection, apply to the order destroyed by sin, that of the old covenant, and should therefore be used — even in marriage services and other liturgies! — only in their New Testament meaning, that is, in the light of the order fulfilled in Jesus Christ, and his church. According to this order, however, the man is not commanded to "rule over" but to "love" (Eph 5:25), and the woman is called, in accordance with her original role (Gen 2:18), to assist him "as his partner." That is her portion of the responsibility for the order which encompasses them both. "His partner": this embraces both — her existence, which is unthinkable without his, and vice versa. That is the promise issued to men and women in Jesus Christ, that in the painful sickness and corruption of their relationship they may know that this complementarity is fulfilled in the relationship of Jesus Christ to his church (Eph 5:22), and that consequently they may live as people who encountered each other in this way "from the beginning." For from the beginning their relationship of complementarity was determined by the "great mystery" (Eph 5:32).

Anyone wanting to understand the relative position of men and women without this "mystery" will necessarily misunderstand the position of women. Anyone who does not know about *the* subjection that occurred then will necessarily regard the position of subjection as an inferior one. They will not appreciate the honor and dignity inherent in this responsibility in particular, namely, women's responsibility. Paul, however, has understood this. He knows that women in their position correspond to the position that Christ, and also he himself as apostle, occupies in relation to their Lord. Admittedly, we are only talking about a "correspondence" here. Yet as such it contains a special promise, and can therefore function as a witness (cf. 1 Pet 3:1). The apostle does not want the church in its assemblies to do without this witness. The church needs it. It needs this reminder of its own subjection. It is not at all the case, therefore, that women are being pushed to one side as less gifted members of the church; rather, they are "needed" in their specially honored position of being, precisely, women. They are summoned to carry out the ministry that only they can carry out, and thus to take note of their particular responsibility. What stands behind the silence demanded of women is not any incapacity to speak in public, but their recognition of their particular task. They too "desire to know," they are "learners" (1 Cor 14:35), "pupils of the Word of God" (Calvin). Recognizing this, they are willing to renounce the exercise of the gifts that they too have received for the sake of a ministry that will build up the church.

Inasmuch as silence on the part of women is counterposed to speaking on the part of men, the boundary of all human speech becomes visible, and the listening church, *ecclesia audiens,* is counterposed to the teaching church, *ecclesia docens.* Who would dare to say that the former is inferior?

## III

The witness, the form of obedience that women should act out, will vary according to different times and circumstances. Therefore, we not only may, but must, ask whether the form of witness demanded by Paul in Corinth in his day is still binding on us in the same way today, or in other words, whether women are still commanded nowadays to remain silent in church.

At all times, and more or less in all churches, this passage from Paul (and also 1 Tim 2:12; see above, pp. 106-10) has been held up to women like a police warning: Here is chapter and verse, you shall be silent! There can be no doubt but that to treat the Word of God in this way is unspiritual and therefore impermissible, whatever one's views on the specific question in hand.

What is deplorable is that by and large women — including Christian women — have responded, and still do respond, not by pointing out that such a use of Scripture is illegitimate, but by rejecting Paul with feelings of anger and alienation for having been led to make such a regrettable pronouncement by his "antipathy to women." Thus we read, for example, in the foreword that Pearl Buck wrote to the German translation of her book *The Exile* (which is a biography of her mother): "For him (my father) she (my mother) was only a *woman*. Ever since those days when I saw her whole being sunk in melancholy (her husband had refused her permission to join in the work of his mission), I have harbored a profound hostility to Saint Paul. And every woman must feel the same because of everything that he has done to women in times gone by . . . proud, freeborn women who nevertheless, simply because they were women, were condemned. For their sakes I am glad that in these new times his power is at an end."

It is not Paul who has "done" things to women — and thank God that we can still hear his testimony in the matter today! — it is his interpreters! One finds some astonishing things in the theological commentaries on 1 Cor 11:3-4 and 14:34. Consider this, for example, in Delling's *Paulus' Stellung zur Frau und Ehe* (in Beiträge zur Wissenschaft vom Alten und Neuen Testament IV/5 [Stuttgart: Kohlhammer, 1931], p. 106), on 1 Cor 11:7: "What is meant is that God and man have a sphere of activity from whose operations their power and glory become apparent, and in particular through the subjection of her whom they influence. As man is a reflection of God, in which God's power and glory become invisible in respect of his roles both as Ruler and as Creator, so too is woman a reflection of man against which the fullness of his power can and should emerge."

It is appropriate to mention at this point that as early as 1902 a theologian like Fritz Barth was calling in a public lecture for the witness of women in the New Testament to be heard, and for people

> at last fully to take into account the specifically Christian notions of women. The common image of women that is

191

current today is at best Jewish but indeed more often is pagan. According to this conception, a woman is a thoroughly dependent being, good enough to satisfy man's lusts, to bring him a rich dowry, to cook well for him, to give him children and then to look after them as well. In society she can, as a polished display object, advertise her husband's good taste and the profitability of his business. . . . She is seldom drawn into her husband's circle of ideas (should he have one), and if she is, her job is always to agree with him. . . . And at the same time women's limitations are a matter of complaint. . . . Yet opinion holds firm that a woman and a stove both belong at home; she is born to serve. Goethe was right when he said, "A woman should learn in good time to serve, according to her destiny. . . ." Fine words — but many a woman has perished as a result of this notion.

Fritz Barth calls for the complete abolition of the notion of women as second-rate human beings, for better training for girls for their future careers, and for a revision of the law insofar as it one-sidedly favors men ("Die Frauenfrage und das Christentum," in *Christus unsere Hoffnung* [Bern: 1913], pp. 156-57).

The apostle's exhortations and prescriptions are not legal requirements; they are living pointers that indicate to us a particular direction and demarcate a specific area within which we today are to hear the advice of yesterday. They are trying to tell us something quite specific still today.

I am not therefore challenging the timelessly valid presuppositions of Pauline teaching: that, within the framework of order determining the relationship between men and women, women are subordinate. I find myself in disagreement, therefore, with a widespread tendency in women's circles today to attack this presupposition and as far as possible to demolish it as a notion that may indeed have corresponded to the position of women at that time but that nowadays is outdated and hence out of place. We would do better (it is claimed) to avoid completely any talk of a difference between the position and function of men and women, for apart from the psychological and biological differences, which are still acknowledged, we should think only in terms of equality in all areas of life. Then, insofar as people retain a Christian allegiance, they happily quote Gal 3:28 and praise the insight bestowed on Paul at that point in contrast to his rather embarrassing utterances in 1 Corinthians.

In order to understand this "progressive" position correctly, we must appreciate that even today women have not faced up to the problem, and, far from independently taking on their responsibility, thoughtlessly conform with the facts as they are, choosing the more comfortable path of a peaceful accommodation with men, not least because it is the latter who are still mostly the ones who set the tone in the social and economic realms. Christian women then like to speak of their divinely ordained "subjection," thus lending to their thoughtless line of least resistance the appearance of having made a conscious decision to be obedient.

Paul's exhortation to women cuts straight across these two possibilities, the "progressive" and the "reactionary." In both cases the concept of *hypotagē*, subjection, gets loaded with preconceptions that do not correspond with the apostle's intentions. In both cases one "knows" from the outset who the men and the women are, and the framework of order in which both have been placed. In both cases one has one's agenda, whether an aggressive or a passive one. It is therefore understandable if some experience the exhortation to subjection as an outrageous unreasonable demand, while others claim it as confirmation of their clueless, and to a considerable extent, ripely bourgeois, indolence. Paul is not interested in these alternatives but in the Christian's compliance with the framework of order in which God has placed men and women, and specifically in women's compliance, because their position corresponds to the position of Christians, of the church, because it acquires significance particularly in the church. For it is here that the natural order first reveals its true

193

meaning and ultimate justification. For only where its fulfillment in Jesus Christ and his church is recognized is it also possible to recognize that the creation of humanity in the duality of male and female is a parable of this fulfillment as an offer of grace. By confronting human beings with fellow human beings from the beginning, and in particular with fellow human beings in the form of a different sex — men with women, women with men — and by making it so that only together are the two truly the humans whom he chose and intended, God created humans not as solitary beings but in the form of beings constituted by an encounter between I and Thou, thus preparing them for the encounter with the human Thou that is at the same time the divine I. This encounter occurs in the church that the Lord himself has chosen as his complementary counterpart.

The complementarity of man and woman can only be an analogue of this quite different complementarity that Ephesians describes as "the great mystery" (5:32). Yet as an analogue, or parable, it can become a pointer to the real thing, and men and women can understand their mutual complementarity in the light of the fulfillment that has come about in Jesus Christ, and each person can recognize the position and function assigned to them as both promise and claim of the divine command. It is precisely their difference in their unity that becomes significant here. Anyone who wanted to doubt that what we have here are not identical partners, but different ones who are not interchangeable at will, and who fit into a determinate framework of order, would not have understood that it is precisely the difference that guarantees the independence of each person and also the equality of their partner. Here each individual has to assume the responsibility that is theirs, for here each individual is challenged by God's commandment in their place and in their position within the common framework of order. Thus here each person has to give their response, which admittedly should be sufficiently in accordance with the other person's that it declares the unity of the human pair. If humanity's existence in the form of men and women is understood merely as a fact to be transcended by humans, as a "situation," then the difference becomes, for women in particular, a tiresome affair that, however, simply should not be taken seriously!

What is really decisive here is that the sexual determination of humans should be recognized as a constitutive and definitive determination of their existence. This in turn will be recognized only where one knows that as part and parcel of the divinely ordained uniqueness of each human being there belongs the fact of being either a man or a woman, and that the promise and the claim of God's command always applies to this sexual determination too. This is indeed the honor of men and women, that it is as such, as men and as women, that they are addressed by God. Where people recognize this, there remains no room for a comparative evaluation.

Seen from this perspective, each person can only find themselves as a grateful creature in their place and no other. Surely a woman who knew this, free of any kind of inferiority complex in relation to men, would relax in great peace — not for nothing is this notion of *hesychia* (quietness) closely linked to that of *hypotagē* (see 1 Tim 2:11ff.; 1 Pet 3:4) — and rejoice in the fact of being, after all, a woman rather than a man. For surely behind all the efforts to play down or even deny the fact of difference there lurks a sense of insecurity on the part of women that their position and function, compared with those of men, may be inferior and therefore disadvantageous. And surely this sense of insecurity springs from a widespread erroneous interpretation of the notion of subjection. Of course, to be subject, to subordinate oneself, *hypotassesthai*, means to assume, within a particular pattern of order, the position of a partner in relation to whom another has priority, means acknowledging this other person in their position and blending into the pattern of order along with them, thereby maintaining this order. Yet who is to say that the position of women, just because it is second place, is one of dependence or indeed inferiority? Certainly not Paul. It is precisely to an independent assumption of their responsibility that he summons women. It is not from men that they receive their instructions, and it is not the wishes or the will of men that constitute the criterion of their decision to obey, but it is the command coming to them from God that fixes them in the position they occupy. What specific decision to obey is demanded of women today, here and now, is not something that can be anticipated, and nothing could be more fatal than to play here with roles and models, be it the model of the *femme libre,* or indeed the model of the "Marian woman," or be it the role of rebel or indeed of the compliant woman and the "eternally feminine." It could well be — and there is much to be said for this — that women today are called to appreciate in a more independent manner than ever before their responsibility in public life and not to leave this up to a mere handful of women from whom, moreover, they end up distancing themselves in practice (for example, in relation to the vote!) with the stupid and always rather coquettish remark: "We are happy to leave that to the men!" That could be the case, but it does not have to be the case in all matters. It could also be that a woman's decision to be obedient in a specific case imposes attitudes of modesty and reserve. Neither the one outcome nor the other can be determined in advance as a matter of principle, nor does the notion of subjection entail that it should. The content of this notion simply cannot be predetermined; all that it indicates is that women should not deny their allotted place in their thought, speech, or action, and that they acknowledge their responsibility for the pattern of order in which they stand together with men.

At this point we return to the specific question that we are concerned with here. Are women still required today to renounce active participation in the ministry of the proclamation of the Word in church? Does the church still today need the witness of their silence, or does it perhaps need a different kind of witness?

We have heard with what degree of richness and variety this proclamation took place in the church's services in Corinth —

and to a greater or lesser extent in all the services of the early church — how the voices of prophets, the stammering of those who spoke in tongues, how psalms and hymns (not to mention the ecstatic celebration of the Communion meal) all got mixed up together, so that it was only with difficulty that the apostle could restrain them and call them to order by reminding them of the need to build up the church as the very aim of the church service, and one that they had to make a priority; for it is not they but the Lord himself who builds up his church through forms of ministry that are rooted in love.

And today? Today the whole congregation is silent, men and women alike, and this silence in church is broken only by a few hymns and, in somewhat more liturgical churches, perhaps also some antiphonal singing before and after the sermon. One man speaks, Sunday after Sunday, and sometimes too on a mid-week evening, proclaiming the Word of God to the congregation. This man has studied theology, has passed his exams, has shown himself to be competent as a probationer or assistant minister, and has now been called and installed by the church to carry out this ministry. He carries it out in the context of church services in considerable isolation, compared with a congregation that, at least judging by appearances, is sunk in almost complete passivity. The richness of earlier voices has disappeared, the action of the Holy Spirit is — at best — confined to this one voice. "Whenever a minister fails in his understanding of faith, or whenever a preacher passes on just one particular message in a very one-sided way, that affects the whole congregation. . . . In early Christianity things were different. . . . In our unfortunate one-man system we have no choice but to influence the whole congregation with our one-sidedness" (Eduard Schweizer, "Die Urchristenheit als ökumenische Gemeinschaft," *Evangelische Theologie* 10 [1950/51] 287). Can silence still be a form of witness among people who do nothing but remain silent? Does the church today still need to have its hyper-enthusiasm dampened, or does it not stand in much greater need of being reminded that *all* members are called to a ministry in the church? Naturally we cannot force the presence of the Holy Spirit and its gifts, but we can and must plead for its coming, and if at all possible refrain from placing too narrow limits on its wide-ranging action from sheer lack of faith on our part (cf. Franz-J. Leenhardt, *Die Stellung der Frau in Neuen Testament,* Kirchliche Zeitfragen 24 [Zurich: Zwingli, 1949], p. 55). Narrow limits of this kind threaten to become part of the understanding of "office" as this has developed in the Protestant churches too.

Faced with this situation, the question arises as to whether the form of witness that women should be offering their congregation in church services today should not be one of speaking, rather than remaining silent as in the church at Corinth, with the implication, of course, that women today may be being called to participation in the ministry of the proclamation of the Word. There can hardly be any doubt, surely, that in view of the dominance in today's church of male clergy and theologians there is an urgent need to recall people to the New Testament understanding of an office as being one of service and ministry. Yet it may be that women can offer a contribution to ministry of a kind that men cannot. Of course, they will be able to make their distinctive contribution only if, in compliance with their position as women, they hear a genuine call to do so. They certainly should not seek to "force" their way into ministerial activities with claims of "equal rights" or "parity of treatment" with men (now deemed to be required within the church as in many other areas of life), nor should they argue that the "feminine contribution" needs to be incorporated here as elsewhere (at least in so far as this refers to an enhanced contribution of a psychological nature!). A woman needs to have a calling to minister, if her participation is to be legitimate. The test of this calling will be that her participation is seen as being necessary for the sake of building up the church, as was women's willingness to remain silent in the time of the early church.

It should be obvious, of course, that the form of witness

offered by women today should not be in the least such as might further reinforce the general passivity found in church. The church today needs a clarion call to active participation, and it may well be, therefore, that the form of witness that women can offer consists in standing forth and speaking out, with a calling to be an active minister of the Word. In situations of emergency, such as during wartime, when men are frequently prevented from exercising their proper office as ministers of the Word, it may happen that women are called to act in their place. Yet times of emergency call forth emergency regulations, not, in principle, endorsement of the new arrangement. That is why the question of women being "admitted" to this office has only seriously begun to be asked (with a few exceptions) since the war, and without as yet reaching an unambiguous conclusion. In fact, in nearly all countries women are engaged in the performance of this ministry, burdened, however, by the sense of uncertainty as to whether in the last analysis what they are doing is legitimate.

Now if it were merely a matter of appointing some female "officeholders" alongside the male, then the legitimacy of doing so would have to be denied, especially in churches where supply exceeds demand. But it is not simply a question of enlarging the ranks of the clergy to include a few women; it is a question of women as ministers of the Word making an essential contribution to a very necessary remodeling of the "office." Women are, by virtue of their natural position in the divinely appointed framework of order, less liable to usurp authority, and therefore as *Verbi divini minister* less liable to be tempted to cast their ministry in an authoritarian mold, meaning, moreover, that they will be less inclined than men to be tempted to allow the authority of the Word to be overshadowed by the authority of their person. Their natural position corresponds, we saw, to that of the church, and thus they will find it appropriate, if they exercise their ministry in a spirit of obedience, to carry out their task as ministers of the Word *in* the church rather than *above* it. They will not come across as aloof but as a link between their office and the congregation, yet without in

199

the slightest degree compromising the authority of the ministry entrusted to them. That is precisely when this authority will be seen to be the authority of the Word, not of the person. "It would be instructive," urges Leenhardt ("Die Stellung," pp. 53-54), "to investigate to what extent the Christian proclamation, and indeed theology and the souls entrusted to the church's keep, have suffered from the fact of an almost exclusively predominance of masculinity. . . . Meanwhile nothing proves that the office of minister, as it has been handled under male influence, is the only form of the office that is either possible or desirable." In quoting this my intention is not to move into the field of psychological observations but merely to underline the significance of the difference in the position and function of men and women for the office of the minister of the Word.

Taking everything into consideration, today women can still but anticipate the final shape that their ministry in proclaiming the Word will take. That will be their opportunity, when they recognize their distinctive task, in other words, when they no longer need to be content with being a never quite successful imitation of "The Vicar," but chart their own course. They will then carry out their ministry as "women in the pew," mindful of the fact that each individual is called to minister with the particular gift each has received. They will respect the gifts of other members in the church and allow them to be fully appreciated and also be sensitive enough to move into the background themselves as and when appropriate. On the one hand, they will not seek anxiously to safeguard a "monopoly" of the proclamation of the Word, and on the other hand they will perhaps want to take on forms of ministry such as were promoted by the "widows" in the New Testament as "good works" (1 Tim 5:10), works of charity. The "remarkable emphasis on the role of the preacher has misled us into seeing the whole of church life as consisting in speaking. The result is that we have pushed doctrine — which certainly is important in and central to the New Testament — into a monopoly position to such an extent that we have completely forgotten that there may be members of the church who, while not being so doctrinally knowledgeable as us, are nevertheless much stronger and more creative believers than we are" (Schweizer, "Die Urchristenheit"). In doing so they will not culpably neglect their central task but will show that it can be carried out only in community and not in isolation, and that no gift is worth anything that is not rooted in love. They may — and this is no small matter — develop their own style in externals too (even avoiding the wearing of vestments?), thereby demonstrating in that respect too that what is important to them is not the tokens of office but the service they are entrusted with providing.

These suggestions are not meant to constitute an actual program of action but merely to highlight the general direction in which women could move, in shaping their ministry, in order to demonstrate and strengthen their solidarity with the church, and to bridge the gap that has opened up between church and clergy. The specific decisions will naturally need to be taken as appropriate according to time and circumstance.

Women are faced with a difficult task whenever they receive a call to the ministry of the Word, and are faced with a virtually impossible one if they are unable to harmonize their ministry with their position as women. They are faced with a "clerical office" shaped in a particular way by men, and initially at least feel constrained to come to terms with this, either by conforming to it as it is, or by altering it in accordance, say, with a newly granted understanding of "ministry." If they find their own way forward, recognizing the task that has been given to them in particular, and bearing in a spirit of obedience the responsibility for proclaiming the gospel correctly, and thus for leading the church correctly in accordance with the divine Word, then they will be able to carry out this ministry in the joyful certainty that they are indeed giving the witness that is demanded of them and that is necessary for the sake of building up the church.

It will be the church's task to reach the practical decision

201

of whether to call women publicly to the ministry of the proclamation of the Word. However, this cannot mean that women should wait around passively for this decision from their respective church leaders. For they too are part of the church, they too are called to share the responsibility for this decision, and are thus by no means merely the object but also and very definitely the subject of this decision.

In conclusion I would like to quote an Anglican theologian, R. W. Howard. He delivered three lectures on our topic to Oxford University. Initially a passionate opponent, he came after a thorough investigation of the whole issue to be an unconditional proponent of admitting women to the clergy. The lectures have since been published under the title *Should Women Be Priests?* (Oxford: Basil Blackwell, 1949). The book ends with an indication that those women who are today doing pioneer work in support of the full "office"

> must have the deep humility and love which will enable them to undertake lowly service that will often seem unworthy of their powers. They must cultivate an unquenchable sense of humour that will help them to smile at the outmoded prejudice of the men and women who will deride or hinder their work. Above all they will need the spirit of true devotion to our Lord Jesus Christ, and to those whom He wills to send them. . . . It may be — surely it must be — that if enough such women can be found to act as pioneers, our Church as a whole will one day come to recognize this devotion and service as a genuine answer to a genuine call from God; a call so clear and unmistakable, that first the Church, and then the bishops, will not dare any longer to refuse to identify the call as being the clear command of the Holy Spirit.